Spirit of the Lights

by Chuck Frederick

Lake Superior Port Cities Inc.

First Edition: October 2011

 Lake Superior Port Cities Inc.
P.O. Box 16417
Lake Superior Duluth, Minnesota 55816-0417 USA
Port Cities Inc. 888-BIG LAKE (888-244-5253)

5 4 3 2 1

Library of Congress Cataloging-in-Publication Data

Frederick, Chuck.
    Spirit of the lights / Chuck Frederick.
        p. cm.
    ISBN 0-942235-11-8
    1. Christmas – Minnesota – Duluth. 2. Christmas lights –
Minnesota – Duluth. 3. Winter festivals – Minnesota – Duluth.
    4. Duluth (Minn.) – Social life and customs. I. Title.
    GT4986.M56F74 2011
    394.266309776'771–dc23   2011021739

Printed in the United States of America

    Editors: Konnie LeMay, Ann Possis, Bob Berg
    Design: Randy Bauer; photography by Dennis O'Hara
    Printer: Sheridan Books Inc., Chelsea, Michigan

For Ellie.
And for Alan, Beverly, Comet, Dan, Dave, Howard, Howard, Jim,
Joe, John, Lorene, Mom, Randy, Shannon, Shirley, Susie, Victor,
Winston Kenmore, and others who left us too soon and who are
remembered every year at the lights.
Also, for everyone drawn to the lights, for whatever reason.
And for Marcia. Of course.

Contents

Preface

"Every year this place warms my heart; it's wonderful, sheer magic. Every year it gets better and as you grow older, Marcia, the magic grows stronger."

This entry in the 2010 guest book brought tears to my eyes. It's hard to understand how a simple love for twinkling outdoor Christmas lights could have had such an impact on so many people.

The year my husband passed away could have been difficult, but focusing on the lights kept me going. Once they were up and ready, I just thought "Why not share them with others by encouraging them to walk through the property."

I've called it the "spirit in the lights" because of all that seems to happen around them.

That first year after Alan's passing, an older gentleman with a white cane asked to speak with me. He said, "I needed to meet you. I needed to tell you that this is the third time that I've been to see your lights. I'm a blind man, and these are the most beautiful lights I've ever seen."

Newlyweds once told me they had their first kiss under the mistletoe hung on one of the arches. Many other entries throughout the years have announced engagements.

One time, a mother and daughter sat in my garden house, and the mother announced that she was celebrating her 90th birthday that evening, Christmas night.

Another time, a young boy, new to the neighborhood, visited each evening with his dog. One night he wrote in the guest book "This is so beautiful, I could live here."

And then there was the 3-year-old who jumped out of the family van giggling and yelling, "I believe!" as she scrambled to my "wishing penguin."

The lights have given me a chance to meet an eclectic mix of new friends from around the world. The opportunity to share my property along the shore of Lake Superior is a privilege for which I am truly grateful.

Now I'm grateful, too, to Chuck Frederick and to everyone at Lake Superior Port Cities for bringing my story … and the stories of those who have visited the lights … out for others to share. I hope these stories – these "spirits of the lights" – are enjoyed and cherished as much as people seem to enjoy the shining pathways found at my home each Christmas.

– Marcia Hales, 2011

from Marcia's Guest Book

Congrats Mrs. Hales,
It is truly astounding that people in this generation of
"fast-paced, screw your neighborism" can still find
trust in fellow man! To take the time and energy to
share your love and joy of the holiday spirit with others
is remarkable and awe inspiring!! This type of
generosity is hopeful and characteristic of God's
original plan!! Thanks,
>   – J and T Siegel, Sioux Falls, South Dakota
>   from the first guest book, 1999

The Coolest – Christian
The Best in the World – Cory
p.s. Good hot chocolate, 2001

This is truly the most wonderful thing I have
ever seen! It is so absolutely beautiful!
Thank you so much for sharing so much.
Peace to you.
>   – Erica Ferich, New York, 2003

1
Donna

Snow whipped across the street as though it was in a hurry. Donna Kennedy certainly wasn't. She pulled at the collar of her coat and at the black-gray vest underneath, wrapping them tighter around her chin. She squinted, protecting her chestnut-brown eyes from the driving storm. She strained to locate her car. Trudging toward it, she wondered how her day – and her life – could possibly get much worse.

Four winters earlier, in her mid-40s, she had slipped on the ice outside Wal-Mart, where she worked in the bakery. Reaching out to catch herself, she jarred her shoulder on the frozen asphalt and jammed her thumb up into her wrist. Her hand was never the same. The pain was constant. It kept her from sleeping. It had been months since she had gotten more than a couple of hours at night, the sleep deprivation contributing to other problems. Unable to carry unwieldy, heavy trays of baked goods, she had to leave the bakery job she loved and take a job at the store as an optometrist's assistant, a job she loved a little less.

Worse, the pain made it impossible for her to paint or to make photographs, her true passions.

The storm in St. Paul two weeks before Christmas was unexpected, but not at all surprising. When it snows, it blizzards, right? Donna had made the trip from her home in Hibbing, Minnesota, a good 3½ hours to the north, to see a hand surgeon. Not that doctors ever helped. She had been to them all, it seemed.

Getting around the Twin Cities was a nightmare anyway because of all the congestion, especially when compared to the ease of getting around her small, iron-mining hometown. The piling, whipping, face-stinging snow made moving and navigating even more difficult. Her car slid off the road and got stuck. Twice. Then her car door froze shut. And a parking spot turned out not to be a spot at all. She stuffed the parking ticket into her coat pocket.

1

Which was where she reached her hand after finally arriving on foot at her car. She just wanted to get in, get warm and get home. But the pocket didn't have keys in it. Her shoulders drooped as low as her spirits at the sudden realization. She had locked her keys inside the car. Along with her money. And after allowing her AAA to expire just weeks earlier because it was a luxury she no longer could afford due to the medical expenses.

"Life can go a little bit out of control, but this was nuts," Donna said later. "This was overwhelming."

Another night in the Twin Cities.

The following morning, with new snow tires purchased first thing, she finally pointed her car north onto Interstate 35. But the drive didn't prove to be the mind-clearing alone time Donna expected, hoped for and needed. Of course not. The lingering storm turned the trip into a stress-filled, white-knuckle crawl.

When she reached the paper-mill city of Cloquet, still about 70 miles short of her back door, she decided she didn't want to go home. Not yet. Rather than exiting and heading north along the highway that led to Minnesota's famous Iron Range, she followed the interstate east toward Duluth, the westernmost and largest port on Lake Superior. The city clings to a hillside bluff above the greatest of the Great Lakes the way a 2-year-old clutches to her mother's leg. Donna headed there, finding her way to Duluth's giant holiday lighting display at Bayfront Festival Park. Lights and cheer twinkled along the rocky shores of the Duluth-Superior Harbor. Christmas lights. That's what she needed. Maybe they could lift her spirits. Maybe she could snap some pictures. She had her camera. Serious photographers always do.

Parking at the city-sponsored display was four bucks, though, and she just didn't feel like digging it out or paying at all. With a deep sigh, she decided to head across the Aerial Lift Bridge instead. Maybe she could get some good pictures of the lights from the opposite shore.

Her tires hummed on the bridge's grated road surface, its crisscross of holes designed to allow snow and rain to fall through.

A funny thing happened on the other side. Donna didn't stop, or even slow down. She didn't look back over her shoulder at the lights spread out in front of the Bayfront stage. She just kept driving. Until she saw, in the distance, a glow.

"It just rose out of nowhere," she said.

"Oh, my," she breathed as she approached. "Is that beautiful."

She pulled over, unable to take her eyes off a full-yard lighting display. She figured she'd snap a few pictures from the road. But then she saw a hand-painted sign at the end of the driveway. Its green lettering on whitewashed plywood welcomed visitors to the "holiday light fantasy."

"FEEL FREE TO WALK THROUGH," the sign read. And, "ENJOY!"

"It was so windy and so cold," she recalled, "but it was so beautiful, too, and so unique, so different. This was not a Menards display with just a bunch of ready-made decorations."

But what was this place? Who in the world created it? And who would allow just anyone to walk through? Donna marveled at the amount of work that had to be involved. "Why would anyone?" she whispered.

Shivering, but hardly noticing it, she shuffled into the yard, her stylishly thin North Face jacket, even thinner jeans and her well-worn, black, leather loafers offering little protection from the elements. A pair of gloves remained in her coat pockets; they were just too bulky for making photographs. She pulled her jacket's hood over her wavy, jet-black hair and made her way through a tunnel of lights and past a waddle of plastic penguins. She paused, firing her Nikon and noticing that the tux-wearing critters huddled around an igloo of lights and a sign. "BELIEVE," the sign read. Donna paused again at a fountain of lights before she spotted a campfire at the center of the yard: a place to warm up. A young man was poking at the flames there and was just about to add more wood.

"Hi there," he said. "Welcome." He said his name was Foster. He and Donna exchanged pleasantries. They talked.

Something surprising started happening. All of the ugliness, the misfortune and the storm-stirred stress of the previous two days began to drain from Donna's thoughts. Even the previous four years were washing away: the pain, the sleepless nights, the frustrations.

Better. That word is quite simplistic, and it isn't very eloquent, but it was the perfect word for how Donna suddenly started to feel.

"You should meet my Grandma," the young man said at last. "Come on. I'll introduce you." He put down his stick and led her toward the house.

A woman with a mop of gray hair and wearing a baggy gray sweater answered the door and immediately ushered Donna inside. "It's so cold out there," she insisted, introducing herself as Marcia Hales. "Coffee?"

The two talked for hours. Donna told Marcia about her accident, her chronic pain and her hellish trip to the Twin Cities.

Marcia told Donna about the lights. So many come now, she said; so many are drawn. "There's magic in the lights," said Marcia.

Donna listened, enraptured. She nodded in agreement and wonder. What had drawn her?

"What Marcia didn't know, couldn't have known, was that I was at one of those crash-and-burn moments right then in my life," Donna said. "She provided a haven for me that night, and at a moment when I really needed it, too. That night, Marcia allowed me to be part of her family, part of her life, and part of her spirit – and the spirit of what she does. I was a total stranger, but I felt this huge connection, like I had just made a lifelong friend. Also, like I had just turned a corner."

It was getting late, almost midnight. Marcia needed to turn off the lights for the night, and Donna still needed to drive an hour and a half to Hibbing. But there was something Donna wanted to do first. She asked Marcia to leave the lights on just a few minutes longer. She wanted to return to the penguins, she said. She had seen another sign there, one she dismissed at first, one promising to make wishes come true.

Donna walked briskly back into the tunnel of lights, pausing at the "BELIEVE" sign. She certainly did, she told herself. She bent down next to the penguin with the other sign – the wishing penguin. She put her hand on its head, surprised at how glossy it felt, like polished marble. Years of wishes and rubs had left the top of the plastic bird as smooth as a George Clooney opening line. She patted and rubbed the head like so many others before her, feeling as silly as nearly every one of them. But she also believed, as she reminded herself once again. *There's magic in the lights.*

"Most people probably make one wish. Well, a genie gives you three, right? So I made three wishes that night," Donna said. The first was for help to manage her chronic pain. The second was for strength to paint again and to make photographs again the way she used to, which was well enough to attract admirers and freelance jobs. And the third – well, the third was a bit too personal to talk about.

Donna climbed back into her car and headed home.

* * *

A couple days later her phone rang. It was the clinic. A test she needed before she could enter a new therapy program had an unexpected opening. Would she take it? Were they kidding? In four years she had grown accustomed to waiting weeks, even months, for tests, procedures and appointments. This test had been recommended by the hand surgeon in St. Paul just a few days earlier.

"Yes, of course, I'll take the appointment."

The test led to physical therapy and occupational therapy treatment at Polinsky Rehabilitation Center in Duluth. The therapists worked together, as a team, and, for the first time since her fall four years earlier, Donna noticed improvement. Within weeks.

"I'm not pain-free, but the therapists helped me to understand more the mechanics of why I have issues and how to deal with those issues. The therapy helped significantly. I can sleep without medication now. I'm in a place where I can function. Amazing."

Her pain under control, Donna started painting again, started rebuilding her portfolio, much of which had been lost to a flooded basement.

She started making photographs again, too, rebuilding her redberryimages.com website and making contacts. Possibilities presented themselves. She was invited to travel with a women's empowerment group to Tanzania to chronicle the group's efforts there. It was her first serious job in years. A photo of a green grasshopper contrasted by the bright yellow veins of a lupine leaf that she submitted to the Minneapolis Institute of Arts was selected for a five-month display. And she made plans for a summertime photo show in the northern-Minnesota, edge-of-the-wilderness city of Ely. People wanted to see her work again!

"As I started to feel better, all the things I wanted to do I felt I could do again. I started seeing opportunities again. I felt encouraged to actively pursue something that has always been a passion for me. Not just as a hobbyist but as a working photographer and artist. It's a process, but doors are opening. I'm really encouraged to be moving in the right direction. And that all started at Marcia's.

"There's something very unique and special about this lady, I've decided since my visit. It takes a special person to give without expecting tangible things in return. She doesn't just have a lights display. There is a generosity of spirit and a warmth that Marcia provides. A comforting. For me, whether it was the penguin or that I was able to sit down and talk with someone at a moment when I really needed to or just dumb luck, I don't know. But I do know this: If I had not stumbled on a place that night where I could find refuge, where I could find friendship, I don't know what might have happened.

"She helped me at a time I needed it – without ever even knowing it. She didn't know I was in crisis. But she was there. I found her."

And she found Marcia's lights.

from Marcia's Guest Book

**I talked to God, and He said you guys
that fixed this have a place
in heaven. Angels.**
– Linda from Sweden, 2005

*Several years ago we came upon this wondrous
sight by accident. Now each year we come,
sometimes with our children, siblings, but we
always look each other in the eye and know there is
love and the true spirit of Christmas. Thank you!*
– Sarah & John Kondratuk, 2003

**Your lights are like stars in the Heavens;
the longer you watch the more spectacular
they are!**
**– Linda & Jerry Everidge
Council Bluffs, Iowa, 2005**

*It's like Candyland but with Christmas lights &
it's what you dream about the night before
Christmas.*
– Andrea L., 2003

2
An Angel

The story went something like this whenever Alan Nylen told it (and he liked to tell it often).

A few weeks before Christmas 1998, he bought a 24-foot ladder. That was the year he and his wife, Marcia Hales, decided to turn their yard full of holiday decorations into something spectacular enough to enter in their hometown Duluth's citywide lighting contest. He was up on that ladder, stretching and straining to place – just so – string after string of twinkling beauty and holiday cheer into the highest branches of the tallest pines.

But then his foot slipped. He grabbed crazily at the pine needles in front of him and then for a metal rung, any metal rung, but to no avail. Down he went, crashing into the frozen yard below.

His eyes pinched tight in agony, a moan escaped from his pursed lips. Flat on his back, he gasped for breath and considered the seriousness of his injuries.

After a few moments, his eyes slit open, life returned to the crumbled heap that was his tall, lanky body. That's when he saw her. In the branches and in the lights above, there was an angel. An all-white angel formed by the lights. "Alan's Angel," as he and Marcia would come to call her.

* * *

Here's how the story really went, according to Marcia.

A few weeks before Christmas 1998, Marcia, a longtime lighting lover and yuletide enthusiast, decided to turn her yard full of holiday decorations into something spectacular enough to enter in Duluth's citywide lighting contest. Her husband, Alan, begrudgingly bought a 24-foot ladder for the endeavor and even more begrudgingly climbed to its top to toss clumps of lights into the highest branches of the tallest pines. After climbing back down, he gave the tree as mighty a shake as he could until some of the strings of lights filtered down and tumbled into the lower branches.

Done, he grunted. And was glad for it.

A few days later there was a knock on the door. A young couple stood in the cold of the evening darkness. The young woman shivered, her hood up, her arms wrapped tightly around herself. She hopped from foot to foot. The young man didn't even have on a jacket. The tattoos on his arms dotted with goose bumps, but he didn't seem to care.

"Dude," the young man said as Alan leaned his head no further out of the warm house than was absolutely necessary to consider his guests. The young man pointed toward the highest branches of the tallest pine. "Is that an angel?"

Alan looked. Marcia joined him. And for the first time they saw it. An angel. Formed by the many lines of lights. "Alan's Angel," as Alan and Marcia would come to call her.

* * *

No matter how it happened, there was little doubt: An angel appeared at the massive, well-known backyard, walk-through holiday lighting display of Marcia Hales and Alan Nylen. An angel.

from Marcia's Guest Book

If a Christmas angel had a name, it surely would be Marcia! Thank you for your wonderful hospitality and spreading the Christmas spirit throughout the community for all to see. If we ever leave this area during the holiday season, we would never forget what you've shared with all of us! Happy holidays.

– Calvin, Brett and Heather, 2003

I used your lights as an example in a Christmas sermon in Germany. Beautiful place! Keep warming the hearts and minds of people as you do and might the lights and warmth of Christmas fill your heart as well. God bless you.

– Michael Furchert
Berlin, Germany 2005

3
Marcia

Up near Hoyt Lakes, amid the mines that produced the ore that created the steel that built the tanks and guns and other heavy machinery that won World Wars I and II, a trickle starts deep in the woods – the St. Louis River.

It meanders through Northeastern Minnesota, spilling against weedy banks, frothing around submerged boulders and roaring over drop-offs large and small. The river alternately races and limps toward Duluth-Superior Harbor, the busiest on the Great Lakes, and into Lake Superior, the largest in the world.

All along its journey, the St. Louis River carries silt and sand, the same material that, over hundreds of thousands of years, and perhaps even longer, created the Duluth sandbar known as Minnesota Point. A seven-mile-long freshwater sandbar, it's the longest on Earth and home to an odd little neighborhood – Park Point.

Just wide enough most of its length for a two-lane road, two lanes of bike traffic, and homes crowded on both sides, Park Point was once a summertime getaway and a place where hay fever sufferers escaped for spring and summertime relief in the days before antihistamines.

Because "the Point" is separated from Duluth's mainland by a shipping canal, there's only one way on and off the finger-looking neighborhood. That's across the Aerial Lift Bridge, not far from Duluth's downtown. The bridge spans the canal between Duluth-Superior Harbor and Lake Superior, and if a big boat is coming, motorists get "bridged," meaning forced to wait, as the bridge's road deck lifts straight up to allow vessels underneath and then lowers so traffic can resume.

Despite the inconvenience, and despite the chilly winds that always seem to be howling in from Lake Superior, the Point has slowly been discovered by the wealthy and elite. Their mansions snuggle into the dunes right alongside the old cottages and the simpler houses of yesteryear, creating an intriguing mix of old and new, past and future, wealthy and not-so-wealthy. Park Point is a neighborhood of contrasts, a neighborhood in transition.

And home to Marcia Hales. Hers isn't one of Park Point's mansions. She lives in a modest yet spacious story-and-a-half beach house, its countertops a whitewashed shade of the towering evergreens outside, its tongue-and-groove walls and ceilings the color of the beach sands after they've been drenched by a Lake Superior wave. From October to January her house fills with the fragrance of simmering apple cider, its fresh sweetness for evenings of visitors to her glowing yard outside. Mammoth vats hum on the stove in the snack-bar island that marries Marcia's kitchen to her warm and welcoming sitting area.

Wide, sliding glass doors, as large as one wall, expose the sitting area to the yard, which isn't much larger than a convenience store parking lot or a Little League baseball infield. In that yard, Marcia has created a spectacle: Her breathtaking holiday lighting display remains tasteful and true despite its growth now to more than 120,000 lights. Visitors are beckoned to not only look at the wildly popular lights but to wander among them, to be a part of them, to allow them to become part of their Christmas traditions. A glowing tunnel begins at the edge of the street, guiding a path past the penguins with tangles of green ribbon decorating each of the critters' necks, a lighted igloo and a "BELIEVE" sign in their midst. The path pauses at a wishing penguin before opening to a towering castle outlined by lines of plastic-encased "rope" lights. A lit gazebo stands to the right. A 20-foot, star-topped tower of lights – looking like something out of "Cinderella" – reaches toward the inky darkness of the night sky to the left. Beyond the tower, the well-decorated path continues toward the frozen sands of Lake Superior. Waves crash and recede, "poosh-sss, poosh-sss," giant ice boulders bob and maneuver, "buh-woosh, buh-woosh," creating a soundtrack of serenity. A campfire crackles at the heart of Marcia's display. Plastic lounge chairs surround the sky-licking flames; plumes of smoke race into the darkness. Long sticks for marshmallows lean against the chairs, waiting. On the opposite edge of the display, lighted bears skate across a frozen pond, the lighted outline of an angel graces towering archways and Marcia's heated garden house-turned-cider house offers a respite and warmth. Fairies fill the trees, joined by Old Man Winter. The lights are white with accents of green.

The entire display looks like something created to win a contest. And it was. At first. But the creation only started out that way.

* * *

"My mother was the decorator when I was growing up," Marcia said, slipping her petite, slightly hunched-at-the-shoulders, 65-year-old frame onto a stool at her snack bar. She sipped at a mug of vanilla-flavored coffee, her voice dripping with a thick northern Minnesota accent, a slow, deliberate way of talking in which "yes" becomes "yaah" and in which many sentences start with "well." Her sandy-silver hairdo may be more silver than sandy these days, and the years may have given her a few new smile wrinkles, but Marcia's bright brown eyes are as warm and commanding as ever. They request full attention.

"When I was a kid, Christmas lights were a big deal," she said. "Back then all they had were those big lights so decorating was really something to do. It was really a project and an achievement."

"Back then" was in the 1950s when the working-class West Duluth neighborhood of Marcia's childhood was home to the People's Brewing Company, Diamond Calk Horseshoe Company, Carsten Coal, a research lab for Oliver Mining and other smoke-spewing, blue-collar industries that nowadays would be referred to as economic engines. Her neighborhood was home, too, to bakeries, barbers and afternoons of ice skating at Merritt and Memorial parks. Short walks took Marcia to school at Merritt Elementary, which has since been converted into apartments; West Junior High School, which was torn down in favor of a new Laura MacArthur Elementary School; and Denfeld High School, its clock tower an icon to this day of a hard-working, close-knit community. It was the kind of place where neighbors watched out for neighbors and where kids had a hard time getting away with anything because everyone knew who they were – and who their parents were.

"I really felt I arrived the year Mom made plywood cutouts of three little girls as part of the Christmas decorations," Marcia recalled. "She hand-painted them and was quite proud of them. They all wore red robes because my sisters and I, we all had red bathrobes. I looked at them; I was so proud."

If there was a plywood cutout depicting her brother, neither Marcia nor her mother really remembers. The cutouts, they said – however many of them there were – went atop the roof over the front porch. That house of her childhood, like Marcia's house now, was about a story and a half tall, so getting the cutouts up there and secured was no easy task. Strings of lights lined the home's easier-to-get-at gutters.

"That was about as far as we ever went with decorating," Marcia's mother, Virginia Nyquist, said, her mind sifting through 90 years of living at the head of the Great Lakes. "We always decorated inside the house, too. But that was just something fun to do. We didn't go all out for prizes or anything. We never entered any lighting contests. We were never that good. Ours were pretty small.

"But we did go around every year to see everybody else's lights."

Every holiday season, the family piled into the car, just like so many families still do today. Addresses of can't-miss displays were listed in the morning's *Duluth News Tribune* and in the afternoon's *Duluth Herald* just as they're in the newspaper every year now. Duluth's hilltop Skyline Parkway was always a bright spot, its decorated houses accented by the breathtaking views of the city lights below. Another highlight was out toward 54th Avenue West in the heart of the West Duluth business district, a remnant of the days when Duluth and West Duluth were separate communities with their own governments, police forces, fire protection and even courthouses.

And, of course, no one ever missed the home of Joe Priley at Eighth Avenue East and Second Street.

Priley was a gardener the way Georgia O'Keefe was a painter. The grounds of the Duluth Civic Center were his masterpiece. He transformed the cracked concrete and scrubby, weed-filled courtyard – overlooked on three sides by the city hall, county courthouse and federal court buildings – into a fireworks show of color and life, using trees, bushes, grass, brick-paved walking paths and flowers. At the heart of the display, Priley nestled a three-tiered water fountain that now proudly bears his name. As it should: Elected and routinely re-elected to the St. Louis County Board for 21 years, Priley solicited $40,000 in public donations for the fountain. In 1965, Priley was named to the Duluth Hall of Fame. In 1970, the Civic Center's circular driveway was renamed in his honor. Also in 1970, the First Lady, Lady Bird Johnson, gave him a commendation for his dedication to beautifying the city.

What the First Lady may not have known was that his dedication to Duluth's aesthetics had started years earlier with Christmas lights at his home.

"Oh, he had the most glorious lights display," Marcia said. "I was just awestruck. There was always excitement at Christmas and getting ready for Christmas. Lights were always part of that. That made a big impression on me."

Although Marcia's mother was the decorator, her father, Howard William Nyquist, "loved Christmas," Marcia remembered. Almost as much as he loved antique guns and collecting them. And almost as much as the passion he found in working on behalf of disabled veterans as a social worker for St. Louis County.

As a boy, Howard William Nyquist suffered from rheumatic fever, which contributed to a heart condition. As an adult, extra weight exacerbated the condition and, in 1976, after battling seven years of illness, he died. He was just 51.

"It was difficult. But because he had been sick for so many years, it was also a blessing," said Marcia, who was 30 at the time and going through difficult times of her own. "I really needed to be strong for my girls."

* * *

In 1964, Susie Ramsay worked the counter at Continental Ski Shop in Duluth. She liked it well enough. The owners, her coworkers and the customers all were friendly and easy to get along with. And the work wasn't bad, helping customers get ready for the slopes. But it was time to quit, she decided, to move on, to do something more. She opened a gift shop on the Skywalk, Duluth's network of elevated, enclosed and, most importantly, heated walkways that connect nearly all the buildings downtown and east toward the hospital district. Susie Ramsay called her new shop Sky's the Limit.

Susie turned her job over at Continental Ski to Marcia, her friend from West Duluth. Marcia was 20 then and just starting out in life. Like Susie, she enjoyed the work at Continental and the people, but, also like Susie, before long, she realized it was time to move on, to do something more.

Marcia's boyfriend had asked her to marry him. He had been a year ahead of her at Denfeld High School, but she didn't meet him until they were both at the University of Minnesota Duluth, where Marcia studied sociology. His proposal came within just a few short months.

And four short months after the wedding, Marcia's new husband was drafted. He enlisted for a four-year term, spending the last year of his enlistment at Fort Carson, just south of Colorado Springs on the edge of the snow-capped Rocky Mountains. He worked as a meteorologist.

When his stint in the military ended, he and Marcia decided to return home. Duluth was a great place to raise kids, they agreed. They arrived just before Christmas with barely enough time to put up a tree, much less decorate. Not that Marcia was in any condition. A little more than a month after the holidays, on January 29, 1969, Marcia gave birth to a daughter they named Nicole. Two years, a month and few days after that, on March 3, 1971, along came baby Ashli.

"Christmas was really big. We always decorated two trees, a big one for the whole family and a little one just for the girls," Marcia recalled of her days as a young bride and new mother. "I always loved having lots of packages under the tree. I did lights all the time my girls were growing up. But mostly all inside. It was a lot of inside stuff for sure."

Happy days didn't last for the young family. When Nicole was 4, Ashli 2 and Marcia 30 – the same year her father died – Marcia's husband, an assessor for the city, announced he didn't want to be a father anymore. Divorce followed, and $125 every month for child support.

"I thought I was June Cleaver like my mom. I thought I was going to stay home and bake cookies. But it didn't work out," Marcia reminisced without any hint of self pity.

She had to support herself and her young daughters, so Marcia went back to work. She sold real estate for 10 years. Then she sold Cadillacs at Krenzen Motors, which was across the street from a Duluth landmark, the bluestone Fitger's Brewery building, a survivor of Prohibition. The historic building, today renovated and filled with shops, restaurants and a microbrewery, survived again when Interstate 35 was built through the heart of Duluth's center. But Krenzen didn't; the dealership was forced to move.

Marcia's car-selling days lasted only about a year. The hours were just too difficult for a single mom.

She worked as a business consultant next; the hours were far more flexible. Business owners would come to her with their problems. "I learned to sit and listen and take notes. And then when they were done, I'd go to the library and research their problem. It worked. I became a computer expert before I owned a computer. I had sort of an eclectic work pattern."

Somehow she managed to fit together all the crazy pieces of her life. That was something at which Marcia would learn to get quite good.

from Marcia's Guest Book

Wonderful display! This is the true meaning of Christmas. My husband, Tom, was Alan's sixth-grade teacher at North Shore Elementary and counselor at Clover Valley. Tom remembers him as his all time favorite student.

– Julie Haug Trevillion,
from first guest book, 1999

Thank you so much for putting on the light show! It's so cheery, it makes you feel that everything is right in life. Thank you again.

– Eva Sevastides, 2003

Thanks for bringing back joy and light to the world! Peace!

– Joe Cermatori
New Haven, Connecticut, 2008

4

Alan

The first time Marcia saw him, he had on a blue suede jacket and blue plaid Pendleton pants. His steel-blue eyes sparkled, a smile never left his face and his dimples were so deep Marcia couldn't help but fall inside. Never mind that Alan Nylen was with another woman, at least at the moment, grooving on the dance floor of the Lyric, a downtown club in Duluth's Holiday Center. His thick brown hair bounced and waved with every move and step. At 6-foot-3, he was at least half a foot taller than Marcia; nevertheless, an impression was made.

"I couldn't help myself. He was all duded up," Marcia recalled with a grin. "But I think it was a bait and switch. I never saw him in clothes like that again. I could never get him to wear anything after that but blue jeans.

"He did kind of sweep me off my feet, though."

Alan asked Marcia out and impressed her with stories of flight (he had his pilot's license), travel (he owned a Corvette and had once driven a BMW motorcycle to Alaska) and adventure (his passions included hunting and fishing).

He grew up on Minnesota's North Shore of Lake Superior in the one-time commercial fishing village of Knife River and was one of five kids, he told Marcia over coffee during one of their many dates. His father, Victor, a sheet metal worker, was from Duluth. At the time of his father's death in 1971, Alan was working as a heating serviceman for the General Heating and Engineering Company. His father died young, at age 47, of a massive heart attack that caused him to lose control of his car as he motored east and out of Duluth along London Road. His father's car missed a curve, crossed the westbound lanes and crashed into a tree on the other side of the street. The Duluth Fire Department rescue squad removed his father's body from the wreckage. A fire engine was called to the scene to flush away spilled gasoline.

Alan was a hard worker, like his father. By age 12, Alan was cleaning septic tanks. While still a teen, he learned sheet metal work from his father and later taught those skills at Duluth's vocational technical school. As a young man, Alan and a business partner installed and serviced air-flow and air-exchange systems, including vents and gauges that measured air quality. They called their business Energy and Air.

Alan was good in school, too, referred to by at least one teacher at North Shore Elementary as his "all-time favorite student." In high school, he took advantage of his height and athleticism and played basketball.

Like Marcia, Alan had once been married. Also like Marcia, his marriage lasted only a short time. He and his wife had a baby, he told her, but the baby died hours after birth and the marriage fell apart soon after that.

"I don't think he ever dealt with the loss of that baby," Marcia said. "After I met him, he had a real soft spot for Ashli. She always had him around her little finger."

Marcia's Ashli had been born on the same day as Alan's baby.

Alan and Marcia quickly became inseparable. She included him in the Sunday evening bull sessions she hosted at her house on the Point. Just a bunch of singles, sitting around, talking for hours until, eventually, somebody, usually Marcia, cooked up a hearty meal, the laughter and good conversation never interrupted.

"They were like a couple of old shoes, those two. Comfortable. Just a comfortable relationship. Right from the beginning," James Snyder recalled of Marcia and Alan. He was among the singles who made up that tight-knit, Sunday-night group. A mail carrier then, James would introduce Alan to the addictive game of golf before retiring as postmaster in Virginia, Minnesota, on the Iron Range.

"There comes a point in most people's lives when you figure out you're just comfortable with each other," Snyder said. "No judging, just accepting each other and who you are. They had that."

Marcia included Alan in her holiday decorating, too. Or at least invited him to participate.

"Alan kind of groused about it at first. 'Why do we have to do this?'" Marcia recalled. "It was a guy thing. He just kind of humored me, you know, as I added lights year after year."

"The decorating was all Marcia," Snyder confirmed. "Alan would hold the ladder. He'd tease her."

Never more playfully than the first year he knew her, 1991, the year of Duluth's famous "Halloween Megastorm."

Just a little snow on the pumpkin that year. No biggie. And that's all it was – at first. Before it ended, though, the storm was the stuff of legend, even in a city and state synonymous with blizzards and whiteouts. Decades-old records fell during three days of blinding white, howling, hurricane-speed winds, and thunder and lightning. More than three feet of snow halted travel and sent cars sliding into ditches. Power outages darkened homes. Principals closed more than 400 schools across Minnesota. More than 500 businesses shut down. In Duluth, an estimated 190 million cubic feet of snow had to be plowed, shoveled and blown away by crews.

Everyone was left with a story. Cars lost under snowbanks. Kids sledding down Duluth's suddenly deserted hillside avenues. Workers stranded. Snowmobilers in full glory. Weddings called off. Births that couldn't be canceled. And trick-or-treating. Did anyone make it to more than just a few houses that year? The storm even clouded Duluth's mayoral election, with supporters of one candidate charging that supporters of the other were plowed out while they were forced to wait.

Marcia's Megastorm story involved 8,000 twinkle lights and a blow-molded plastic star inside which she placed another bulb. Even before moving into her house on the Point, she had decided the star would be perfect, absolutely perfect, atop a 5½-foot-tall pine tree near the front door. The rest of the evergreen she wrapped in lights. Around the house, from the gutters, she hung icicle lights, which were new that year and couldn't be kept on the store shelves.

She got it all up early. Too early. She finished decorating just a few days before the Megastorm hit. The blizzard knocked it all down.

"So much for doing lights," Alan gently joked. Marcia seethed. Then put it all back up again.

And again the year after that, adding more lights, a pair of plastic, stand-in-the-yard penguins and a trio of lighted geese. They all found a home in the yard amid the glow of the light-laden evergreen. The penguins and geese were gifts from Marcia's mother. A torch was passed that Christmas.

"I bought myself my first two deer that year, too," Marcia recounted. About four feet high, the deer were actually just the frames of deer, made of resin piping ready to be covered with lines of lights.

"I remember sitting in the basement, putting on the lights and thinking, 'What idiot would do this?' It took me three hours to wire one deer."

For at least 10 years, the Autumnal Equinox Beach Party was a raucous, can't-miss event, an annual happening on Park Point. And wholly unsanctioned, even though Marcia and Lance Reasor, its two main organizers – the ones who bought the kegs of beer, set everything up on the sandy shores of Lake Superior and some years even flew in live lobsters from Maine – were active with the Park Point Community Club.

The party ended in 1994 when Alan decided he didn't like the idea. He considered the combination of booze, the largest – and perhaps coldest – freshwater lake in the world, and the need and desire of some to get home after the bash, and he saw trouble. A disaster waiting to happen. And maybe a lawsuit to follow.

"You're not doing it," he told Marcia.

She stood her ground. "The hell I'm not!" she balked. "This party is the last 'me' thing I have, the last thing that's mine – not ours, but mine. If you think you're going to take it away from me, you're either going to have to marry me or I'm going to have to start looking at other options."

"We can do that," Alan replied, and for a moment Marcia wasn't sure whether he meant they could look at other options, which, really, she didn't want to do, or whether he meant they could get married, which she did want. Finally, he added, "We can go to Vegas at Christmas; do it then."

Marcia was thrilled. But still furious.

"Christmas isn't soon enough," she blurted.

So on September 23, 1994, the day of the autumnal equinox, with the sun crossing the celestial equator, a party on the sandy shores of the largest and perhaps coldest freshwater lake in the world was indeed held. But not to mark another change of season. This celebration marked a new life together, husband and wife, Marcia and Alan. Friends and family filled the back yard of the Park Point beach house the couple would share. They ate cake and hot sandwiches and toasted Marcia, who wore a long-sleeved, white sweater over a ruffled, knee-length, white dress, and Alan, duded up once again in a button-up white shirt, the top button left loose, and a new pair of jeans bought for him by his new bride. A smile never left his face. His dimples were never so deep.

from Marcia's Guest Book

This had been the worst day ever.
Coming here and enjoying your
hospitality has renewed my sense of ...
well, made me feel better at least, which
is saying something. Thank you.

— Unsigned, 2003

*After spending the day at St. Mary's
hospital visiting both my parents, this was
a real pick-me-up. A wrong turn and
lucky glance led us here. It's indeed a
Winter Wonderland! Thanks for sharing.*

— Cheryl Collison
Apple Valley, California, 2000

Wow, this is amazing. It has made a memory
in my life.

— Tammy Tucker
Williston, North Dakota 2004

5
Politics

Marcia was a community organizer and a neighborhood activist when it was just something done to give back, because that's what it meant to be an engaged part of where you lived and because, well, because neighbors needed you to. This was back before any presidential candidate suggested such roles could be touted – or should be. After serving as Park Point Community Club president, and after being a regular at Central Hillside Community Club meetings, running for City Council "just seemed a natural progression," said Marcia, explaining her entrance into local politics. "Also, I had time to do it." The Christmas decorating season lasted only a few months.

The city's daily newspaper, the *Duluth News Tribune*, once described the diverse area of her middle-of-the-city 3rd District as where "poverty and economic growth coexist uneasily." In 1995, the district had a need: Councilor Chris Dahlberg had stepped down to fulfill his obligations as an Army Reserve officer.

Marcia stepped up, urging fair-housing practices and the growth of homeownership to strengthen the city's tax base. She faced little competition and easily won the seat, facing immediate questions about mall expansions, street and sewer repairs and waterfront development, the most pressing issues then challenging Duluth. She faced those and other issues head-on, always head-on.

And she started taking seriously her holiday lighting display, adding more lights every year until, in 1998, with 15,000 lights, including 20 sets of icicle lights around her house and garage, she decided to enter the city's annual holiday lighting contest.

"We've got some neat trees. What the heck?" Marcia said to Alan. "Let's see how we stack up. Let's enter."

Because she was an elected official, she entered under Alan's name. "You're going to be so surprised when you win," she teased.

Marcia spent that autumn testing lights and putting up line after line, even decorating some of her taller trees. Alan bought her that 24-foot ladder. And climbed it again and again the year of the visit from the angel – and the multi-tattooed dude.

Using chicken wire and nine-foot poles, Marcia built a massive "NOEL" sign. Bending PVC pipes, she built four arches and strung lights on them, across them and over them to create a glowing tunnel toward the beach. She pounded six-foot garden stakes into the ground, added I-hooks at the top of each, ran wires to the ground and then wrapped lights around the wires to simulate a forest of twinkling, snow-covered trees.

"Why I did that I am not sure," she chuckled, "I had a lot of trees out there I still could have decorated."

Her deer and penguins and geese returned to the yard, amid the trees both real and simulated. In some of the trees, the real ones, she hung lighted, four-foot snowflakes.

"I really dug in," she said.

At City Hall, she submitted her entry form – er, Alan's entry form.

"That's enough lights," Alan would announce every morning before leaving for work at Jamar, a construction and manufacturing facility where he was plant manager.

"Oh, yeah, yeah," Marcia would quickly agree – before spending another day buying more and putting up more. There was always more that could be done. The ideas never ceased.

In the end, though, it wasn't enough. Debbie and Dan Streu, who, for 15 years had been among the Duluth area's elite lighters, took top honors that Christmas in the city contest's residential division.

"Our nativity scene is probably the best part of what we do. We feel that's what it's all about," Debbie Streu told reporters after accepting her award from Mayor Gary Doty inside the oak-paneled Mayor's Reception Room on the fourth floor of City Hall. "We love doing it."

Alan accepted his plaque for second place and invited Marcia to speak to the media. "He bought the ladder and the lights. I put it all up," Marcia said. "I spent months at Menards figuring it all out. I ought to buy stock in that place."

Walking out of City Hall, Alan suddenly turned to his wife. "Second place," he grumbled. "When you're lying in the ring at the end of the match, they don't give you a prize for second place. We'll just have to work harder next year. We can do better."

We? Do better? Had Alan finally caught the thrill, the competition – and the tranquil beauty – of lighting for the holidays? Marcia wondered. And was thrilled by the possibility.

* * *

The next morning, the addresses of the contest's winners and entrants were published in the *News Tribune*. That evening, lines of cars started inching past the brightest of the houses. Limos and buses led the way, their passengers gawking in wonderment, no one in any hurry. Families in cars and minivans joined the ogling, just like Marcia's family in their car all those holiday seasons earlier.

"Here come the tourists," Alan would announce as the sun went down on the other side of Minnesota Avenue and across the Duluth-Superior Harbor and the Blatnik Bridge.

The viewing was different at Marcia's and Alan's. The couple decided to place a sign at the edge of the road, beckoning visitors not just to drive slowly by but to stop their cars, to hop out, to walk around a bit.

"Welcome to our holiday light fantasy," their sign read. "Feel free to walk through the display. Enjoy! Please watch your step."

The sign didn't say it, but visitors also were welcome – encouraged, even – to huddle around a campfire Marcia built in the center of the display and to stop in the heated garden house for a sugar cookie and a cup of cider, the simmering aroma of apples hauled out a mammoth vat at a time from Marcia's kitchen.

Talk about building community.

"Some nights I think you need a tanker truck for all that cider," Alan joked.

And some nights they did.

from Marcia's Guest Book

ขอบคุณมากๆ สำหรับความรู้สึกดีดีๆ ที่ส่งให้ลูกเทาๆทุกๆคน ♡ น่ารักมากค่ะ

Thank you so much! I love the lucky penguin and unicorn.
— แอ้ม Amp (Bangkok)

That's a wonderful place! I will take a lot of nice pictures with me back to Brazil!

— Daniel
Brazil 2004

Wonderful. Magic! Muito bonito!
— Pualo and Vilma
Coimbra, Portugal, 2004

多謝！祝你身體健康！
Thank you! Wish you health forever and happy forever!
I love your lights.
傑 Kit. (Hong Kong)

An absolutely magical experience; you've completely started my year in the right way.

— Hamish from Australia, 2008

6
Unplugged

Rudy was an exchange student from Germany, attending college in Duluth. He was nearly as tall as Alan. If they were on a basketball team, he'd play forward and Alan center. His nest of sand-colored hair tended to curl into a snarl at the top. When he was being serious, he reminded Marcia of a younger version of the actor Russell Crowe.

Marcia and Alan had met Rudy at Sky Harbor Airport, a single-runway and float-plane facility at the end of Park Point. Alan flew in and out from there. Marcia occasionally helped run the place. Rudy and Alan came to enjoy drinking beer together, staying up late at night and singing "America the Beautiful" and other patriotic songs. Men can be odd that way, Marcia always thought.

Rudy was among the throngs who visited the lights that first year. He entered the house, poured himself a cup of coffee, frowned when he realized it was cold, popped open the microwave, put the cup inside and started pressing buttons. Beep, beep-beep, beep, and then he hit the green "START" button. But instead of the hum of a microwave, he was met with darkness. Total and complete darkness. With all the decorations and lights outside, running an appliance inside like a microwave was just too much for Marcia's and Alan's electrical system.

"You can't just do that," Marcia chided, grabbing a flashlight and heading toward the fuse box in the basement. "You just can't."

Rudy's words followed her down the stairs and gave her pause: "America, what a strange place. You invite all these people to see your yard and you can't cook for a month – or even heat up a lousy cup of coffee."

Strange, yes. And inconvenient, too. Marcia grinned. She wouldn't have it any other way, she decided then.

from Marcia's Guest Book

Thank you! Thank you! What a wonderful thing to do. We came to Duluth for a very sad occasion, but finding this enchanting place helped in this time of grief. Here is to Leah.
    – Laurel Zoet, Sheldon, Iowa, 2003

Thank you for you beautiful display and hospitality. Merry Christmas, Semper Fi
    – USMC, the Kohlmeyers
    Texas, 2006

Thank you so much for what you have done!
    – Sr. Gotharda
Tanzania, East Africa, 2006

*The beauty lies in the tranquility –
thank you for the beautiful, peaceful time.*
    – Unsigned, 2003

7
Good-bye Too Soon

Marcia and Alan spent little time "lying in the ring" at the end of the 1998 match. They leaped into planning for '99. More lights. That was a no-brainer. There were plenty of trees in the yard between the house and the beach that could be lit up. But to win that elusive first-place prize in the city lighting contest, one of the most prestigious anywhere, they knew they needed a "wow," something that would set them apart, identify them and make their display unforgettable.

So Marcia sat down with pencil and paper and sketched out that something. Her drawing looked fancy, elegant and straight out of "Cinderella." The large, looping wheels at the base of her creation resembled the curled-up toes of a leprechaun's shoes. She drew a wheel-shoe for each direction: north, south, east, west. An Eiffel Tower-type structure rose from the center of the wheel-shoes with shooting stars blasting from its midpoint. That tower would support a circle of hooks, each tipped upward so they pointed toward the sky. Marcia added a crown atop the hooks with more stars launching straight into the air from it. At the very top was, of course, the largest star of all.

"The whole thing should be at least 20 feet tall," a breathless Marcia explained to Alan. "Can you build it?"

She knew he could. He was a whiz with sheet metal and with bending and forming metal pipes. She could paint it white and cover it with clear, twinkling Christmas lights, just as she had done with the many frames of deer in the yard.

"We can do that," Alan said.

But he never got the chance.

* * *

For years, Alan joked with co-workers that his birth certificate came with an expiration date. His father died of a heart attack at age 47. At least one other male relative did, too.

"When I turn 47," he teased, "watch out."

But Alan, at 47, with the exception of being a smoker, was fit and healthy. He ate right; Marcia made sure of that. He golfed often, a regular at Ridgeview Country Club, even if it meant wearing fancy polo shirts. He had just weeks to go before turning 48 in mid-August.

"But family history can be a bad thing. It can be pretty spooky," said Rob Link, owner of Jamar Co., the nearly century-old plant where Alan worked his way up to manager. "He'd make light of it, but in the back of my mind, I always thought he was really worried about it. How couldn't you be?"

In the spring of 1999, Alan also was worried about an 18-month contract he was overseeing at Jamar. Under extremely precise specifications, the plant was building storage tanks for a petroleum company. A special kind of steel was needed that had to be imported from Denmark. Twice, as it turned out. The first shipment rusted in Jamar's yard before it could be used.

"He called that contract 'the killer job,'" Marcia said. "He was a perfectionist. He didn't sleep the whole time because he was agonizing over all the details. It was a huge project. He would stay up at night with plans and changes and with figuring out how to fix problems."

The third full week of April, however, the contract was completed. The tanks were delivered. The killer job was over.

And the following morning, the Alan Nylen who headed out the door for work wasn't stressed and on edge. He was relaxed and relieved.

"Wait," Marcia called after him. She gave him a kiss and a small hug. "Love you. Have a good day."

"Love you, too," he said. They were the last words he ever spoke to his wife.

* * *

In his office on the fourth floor of City Hall, Duluth Mayor Gary Doty was finishing up some paperwork before heading home for the day. Square-faced and graying at the temples, Doty contemplated a jog after work. But then his phone rang. It was St. Mary's hospital.

"We need to reach Marcia Hales immediately," pleaded an urgent voice.

"She's downstairs, in the council chambers. The City Council is holding a committee meeting this afternoon," Doty answered. "She's busy. Can I help?"

"Yes, please go and get her. Her husband has suffered a massive heart attack. She needs to get here right away."

"How bad is it?" Doty asked, falling into his high-backed, leather chair as though he had been punched; his voice turned quieter.

"She needs to get here right away."

In the council chambers, Marcia had just asked a question of the city attorney. They were discussing Spirit Mountain, the ski hill and recreation area in western Duluth that regularly was debated by the council because of its city ownership – and its ongoing city subsidy. The mayor walked in, hurried to the front of the chambers and whispered to Marcia, "I need to see you in the hallway."

"All right," she said, "as soon as I get an answer to my question."

"No, now; this is more important," Doty said, and there was something in his tone and face that caused Marcia to get up and follow him out.

Doty drove like a madman down Second Street to St. Mary's. All Marcia knew was Alan had been taken to the hospital and that the situation was urgent. That's all Doty would tell her. Not that he knew much more.

She burst through the hospital's front doors and was grabbed immediately by a pastor or priest or some sort of clergyman. Marcia didn't really notice and didn't really care. She was too perturbed. Why was this person talking to her? Why had he stopped her from seeing her husband? She wanted to get to Alan. "Where is Alan?" she cried, cutting the pastor-priest off in mid-sentence. Then she listened to him for the first time.

"I'm sorry," the cleric said, clutching both of Marcia's hands. "He's gone."

A few moments had to pass before Marcia understood that "gone" didn't mean "released from the hospital" or "headed home," that "gone" meant gone, as in dead.

It took even longer for the details of what happened to make any sense to her. Alan had been complaining all afternoon of indigestion, of heartburn, she was told. But he always was complaining like that, she argued. He was famous for popping anti-heartburn tablets. All the time.

But this time was different, she was told. At the end of the day, he was walking out on the floor of the sheet metal shop to talk to workers when suddenly he just crumpled to the ground.

"His face just went blank. It was like he just shut off, like somebody hit him in the back of the head and knocked him over," Mike Ellis, one of Alan's employees, recalled later. "He was walking right toward me. His heart just gave out and boom. He just fell right over."

"It was so final," Marcia said. "I can say this now even if it sounds callous. If he had to die, it was better that he died right away. Alan would not have enjoyed being a sick guy.

"But it wasn't fair. He was just 47. He was my younger man," she said. "I was lucky to have the years I did with him."

Marcia felt sick. She wanted to leave the hospital. She wanted to go home. She just wanted to go.

She turned away from the cleric with every intention of doing just that.

"No!"

The voice belonged to Isobel Rapaich, elected to the City Council with Marcia in 1995. They were about the same age, were both from West Duluth, and they suddenly shared another bond.

Twenty years earlier, Isobel's husband was on "the fishing trip of a lifetime," as she called it, a trip to Canada he and his friends had been planning and talking about and dreaming about since they were in kindergarten, a trip never far from her husband's mind during their 28 years of marriage and while they were raising four children.

"He and his friends used to argue what heaven was. My husband always said it was going up north to Canada fishing," Isobel said.

In 1979, Dan Rapaich of West Duluth's Raleigh Street – a place famous for toughness and for how fiercely it protected its own – finally made it. He was in the boat on a remote Canadian lake when he suffered a sudden heart attack. His buddies got him to shore as quickly as they could and onto a puddle-jumper prop plane that took him to a hospital. But not quickly enough. He died on his birthday. He was 51.

"I never got to say goodbye," Isobel said, stepping in front of Marcia, heading her off before she could flee. "It's OK to go in. It's OK to say goodbye. Later, you'll wish you did. And he'll know you're there. I never got the chance. You shouldn't miss yours."

Marcia did finally go into the room where Alan was. Accompanied by Isobel and the mayor, she joined Rob Link and others from work. They shared hugs, condolences. And they sat in silence; their heads hung low, their hands folded.

Five days later, the Westminster Presbyterian Church filled to overflowing with others who sat in similar silence, their hands also folded. The church filled with happy memories, too.

"Alan was a great guy and really good at his job. Very smart," said Mike Ellis. "I had just started working for him and that was when we were adopting our son from Colombia. I couldn't afford to lose time away from work, and I didn't have vacation time yet. But Alan let me go – with full pay. He said to me, 'I'm going to take care of this for you.' That was awesome. He was great to work for. Very fair to his people. He did a lot for me. He did a lot for the company.

"His death was hard on a lot of people. He had a lot of pressure. The company was making changes and expanding and expanding," Mike continued. "That was rough on him. His smoking obviously didn't help, either. He smoked like a chimney, one right after the other. But he certainly was under a lot of pressure."

Doing the Christmas lights had become an outlet for Alan – but wasn't enough of a stress relief, Mike said. "That did come to be one of his passions. He came to love (decorating) even if he really didn't at first. Him and Marcia both. He worked hours on end. I went a couple times to help him with that."

Mayor Doty was among the many at the funeral who came to say goodbye and just to be with Marcia. "I did about all you can do, what you normally do," Doty said. "I hugged her and kept quiet and just let her grieve and let her cry. There's nothing you can say other than you're sorry. There are no words.

"Marcia and I weren't the greatest of allies, but politics are politics and people are people," Doty said. "Whatever differences we had were political; they weren't personal."

Jamar shut down for the day. Mike Ellis was far from the only employee who wasn't going to be at work anyway because of the service. Alan was that well-liked at the company.

And was that critical to its success, Link recalled. Alan played a key role in 1988 when Jamar outgrew its space in Canal Park and moved into a new building in a new industrial park in West Duluth's historic Oneota neighborhood, the site of one of Duluth's earliest pioneer settlements. Jamar was one of the first, if not the first, of Canal Park's heavy industries to leave, signaling the waterfront district's 20-year transformation into the heart of Duluth's now-booming tourism industry. Old factories and warehouses were converted one by one into waterfront hotels, wood-floored shops and trendy restaurants, all in the shadow of the iconic Aerial Lift Bridge.

"He was a great guy. He had his ups and downs in life as a lot of people do. He was a very good friend as well as an employee," said Rob Link. "Al was a special one. He did everything with passion, including the holiday lighting displays and golf and all kinds of other things he got involved with, especially later in life. Al took his work very seriously.

"His death was an absolute shock to everybody. He had been taking care of himself and was really looking forward to a great future. And even though he was always half-joking about when he was going to die, I still think he kind of talked himself into it.

"And that would be just like Alan. He always accomplished what he set out to do."

from Marcia's Guest Book

Dearest Marcia and Shirley,
You have the most wonderful house I've ever seen.
The lights were spectacular and the beach took my
breath away. I could spend eternity here and be
forever content. Thank you so much for sharing and
for being such a splendid woman.

> – Helen, a University of
> Minnesota Duluth student, 2007

Dear Shirley,
Your lights are very pretty! Thank you for sharing
them with us.

> – Hallie, Matthew and Lee Klein, 2007

**This is very smart and nice. I like that
you are helping dogs everywhere.**
> **– Dog helper from St. Paul, 2003**

Shirley, I hope you get enough money to help your
friends at the Animal shelter!

> – Love, your friend, Abigail Gilbert, 2003

8
Shirley

A few days after the funeral, still numb, Marcia pushed her way inside the Duluth Animal Shelter, a squat, concrete-and-block building at the foot of 27th Avenue West in Duluth's working-class Lincoln Park neighborhood. The structure's walls and floors were as hard and as gray and as cold as her mood. If the sewage-treatment plant across the street was letting off a stink, as it sometimes did, she didn't notice as she hurried through the chill toward the door. Life stunk enough already.

She had been volunteering at the shelter about a year, cleaning out kennels and cat cages and performing other chores as needed. In charge of the City Council's Public Safety Committee, which was working with the Humane Board to rewrite the city's animal control ordinance, she had become keenly aware of the shelter's many needs. She had become a shelter regular and one of its fiercest advocates.

Marcia was greeted by sobbing. A little boy was curled up on the floor in the center of the shelter's front room. He clutched a shaggy, gray-and-white bearded collie that struck Marcia as familiar. The dog was nearly as big as the boy and resembled the wooly-haired Old English Sheepdogs with which people are more familiar. He held her tight.

"What's the matter? How come you're not in school today?" Marcia asked, crouching down.

His arms still around the dog, the boy managed to rub one fist at his left eye and then his right. He looked up, guardedly.

"My mom said I could stay home," he whispered between sobs. "We're h-here because we h-have to put Shirley to sleep today."

Shirley.

Of course.

Marcia knew the dog was familiar. It belonged to Duluth Animal Control Officer Carrie Lane, the woman who ran the shelter. Carrie sometimes brought Shirley in with her and once told Marcia all about the dog and its many brushes with death – and its precarious prospects for living at her house much longer.

Shirley was born in or near Thunder Bay, Ontario, in the summer of 1988, the same summer Tom Hanks was "Big" and Bruce Willis refused to "Die Hard." The dog was found along the side of a rural road, in a box, with the rest of a litter. She was taken to the pound, survived, and then survived again by being adopted.

Four years later, Shirley was living in Duluth, in a duplex. A neighbor upstairs was worried about her. She could hear Shirley crying at night and yelping at other times, as though in pain. She saw blood once and wondered whether Shirley was being abused. She called Duluth Animal Control, sending Carrie to the apartment.

"The guy who answered the door seemed nice enough, and Shirley seemed happy enough. We talked. There really wasn't anything to do," Carrie said.

A couple of weeks later, though, the guy called.

"The dog seemed to like you," he said, and Carrie smiled, remembering how Shirley, a big ball of fuzz and energy, had jumped up on her when they met, her tail wagging as fast as an umpire's brush sweeping off home plate. "You want her?"

It was Carrie's birthday. She had just received another gift.

But a gift in need of immediate, life-saving care, she quickly learned. Shirley had a bladder infection and pyometra, an infected uterus. She had to eat special, prescribed-by-a-veterinarian meals for a full year. If her previous owner hadn't given her away, Shirley probably would have perished.

If the dog was a gift, the gift turned out really to be for Carrie's then-6-year-old son, Ryan. Shirley quickly became his dog and his closest childhood friend.

"Go wake up your boy," Carrie would tell Shirley in the mornings, and Shirley would scramble toward Ryan's room, her paws awhirl on the linoleum, her excited legs scrambling to keep up. She'd leap up on Ryan's bed and then on Ryan, squirming all over him and licking him until he was awake and willing to surrender.

"It was actually a pretty horrible way to wake up," Ryan said, years later, laughing at the memory. "Shirley was the coolest dog I ever knew. She was always happy. And she always made me happy. Even as a kid. It was hard to be depressed around Shirley."

The dog spread joy all around Duluth's hillside neighborhoods. The back door didn't always latch tight when Carrie and Ryan went out, and Shirley learned how to take advantage, using her nose to lift and slide open the dead bolt. Free, she wandered about, playing with kids, visiting the corner beauty shop and stopping to greet anyone who happened to be up and about.

"I'd get home and she'd be missing and I'd have to call around to see where Shirley was playing," said Carrie. Those were particularly embarrassing phone calls. As animal control officer, Carrie was the one who spent her days catching strays.

On summer evenings, Carrie and Ryan took Shirley to Chester Park for outdoor folk or acoustic concerts. But Shirley always bolted for the park's playground, so turned on by its super-tall, twisting slide that she'd rush past children waiting in line and beat them up the ladder to the top of the slide for the thrilling swoosh back down to the bottom.

"For hours and hours, she'd push her way to the slide," Carrie said. "It was like having an out-of-control kid at Disneyland."

Shirley liked to crawl into people's laps and wrap her arms around their necks like she was hugging them. She always waited to be hugged back.

She once nearly got Maced by a substitute mail carrier who initially mistook her jubilance for an attack.

"Another time I came home and she was in the neighbor's yard," Carrie remembered. "Kids came running up to my car. 'The fire department was here! The fire department was here!' Oh, no. Shirley could climb anything – or would try. That day she was upstairs where we left her and saw through the window that kids were outside playing. She loved kids; sometimes they had snacks, right? So she tried to climb through the open window to get to them. But she got stuck. She wound up hanging there from the window screen by her hind legs. The kids saw her and found a dad with a ladder but the gate to my yard was locked."

So the fire department had to be called, and Shirley had to be rescued, saved once again.

"She was always all full of energy. She was like a pogo stick. She would stand and just jump straight up," Carrie said. "You know what they say about beardies: They die in mid-bounce. She lived pretty happily with us."

As long as no one – especially no other animal – messed with her food. Carrie brought home a kitten from the shelter one night and the little ball of fur and Shirley, a giant ball of fur, got along marvelously. They played some and left each other alone some. The evening went well. But then the kitten snitched from Shirley's bowl. Shirley pounced, biting the kitten's tiny head. The animal died.

"I was a little alarmed, but I forgave her," Carrie said.

Carrie got married, and, from the beginning, her husband was far less forgiving of Shirley. She could be a barker, more and more so with each passing year. Plus, she never did shed the habit of running through screen doors and screen windows. It was as though she had forgotten all about – or didn't care about – that time the fire department had to come. And she definitely was hyper. Always had been. She was nothing like the mild-mannered, sweet-as-creamery butter shih-tzu/poodle, or shih-poo, Carrie's husband brought to their marriage.

Carrie once talked to Marcia about taking Shirley. Marcia considered it. She took the dog to meet Alan, knowing it would be a tough sell. Not long before, Alan had wanted to adopt a springer spaniel. His beloved springer Winston Kenmore had died at age 8 and he had found another, about age 7. Marcia discouraged him. "Why do you want such an old dog?" she implored. She wasn't surprised when Alan took one look at the scraggy and scruffy Shirley and said, "What the hell is that?" She was less surprised when, after Marcia told him Shirley's entire, remarkable and tragic life story, including Carrie's husband's growing intolerance, Alan said, "Are you sure you want such an old dog?" Marcia backed down, just as Alan had done.

Inside the shelter, Marcia hurried over to a desk, plucked tissues from a box and returned, crouching back down beside the boy and his dog. The tissues went unused as tears streamed down the boy's face and into the dog's fur. He refused to let go.

Marcia finally spoke. "Did you say you have to put Shirley to sleep today? But why? What happened?"

"I can answer that," Carrie said, returning from the back, where she had been procrastinating, not wanting to do what she needed to do, what she had come to the shelter to do.

Their shih-poo, she explained, had made the mistake of snitching from Shirley's dish. And for the second time in her life, Shirley had pounced. The Shih-poo lived – in fact, was hardly hurt at all. But the damage was done. Shirley's fate was sealed.

"We love her. We're absolutely heartbroken," Carrie said. "We don't know what to do, but we know Shirley can't live at our house anymore. She's 11. Beardies don't usually live much longer than this anyway. She's had a good life, right?"

"Yes, and she's going to continue to have a good life," Marcia said, and for the first time since he saw Marcia come in, Ryan looked up and eased his grip on his dog.

"What would you think of Shirley coming to live with me?" Marcia said to the boy, not really thinking, just reacting, just doing what she felt needed to be done. "I live on Park Point, on the beach side. She could run in the sand. And you could come visit her any time. What do you say?"

For a moment, Ryan didn't say anything. Finally noticing the tissues in his hand, he wiped his eyes and cheeks. He stifled a sob and sat up a little straighter.

"Really?" he finally asked. "She could live with you? And I could still come see her?" As hard as it was, Ryan realized, too, deep down, Shirley couldn't stay at his house any longer. She had become unpredictable. She had shown she could be dangerously aggressive with other animals.

"Really," Marcia answered, grinning for the first time in days.

"Mom?"

"Sure. Of course."

"I think that sounds like the most perfect idea in the world," Ryan said. "The beach is about Shirley's favorite place of all places. I can't think of anything that could be better for her. She loves to swim, you know. We have to make her stop sometimes when we take her. Once we even had to go out and get her – and even then we could hardly get her to come out of the water."

Ryan, Carrie and Marcia laughed. Shirley barked, having no idea how close to death she had come, once again.

from Marcia's Guest Book

Thank you for this magical, blessed Christmas. It's an answer to our prayers as this past 6 months we lost our father and youngest sister. We prayed earlier today that they could be with us and they are. Thank you. God bless you.

> – Deb & Gordon Bourne
> Canton, South Dakota, 2003

Al would be very pleased of the work you have done; it is truly beautiful. I just want to say that Al is missed very much by myself and many others.

> *– Mike Ellis*
> *night shift shop foreman Jamar, 1999*

I came here 2 years ago, met you & the amazing dog – good conversation – and then I walked on your crunchy beach & had a reunion with my dear departed Mom & Dad, with whom I had walked many beaches in California. It was awesome. ... Happy holidays

> – Lori Greenstein
> Sun City Grand, Arizona, 2003

9
Losses

In her grief and while going through Alan's things, Marcia came across the piece of paper, the drawing, the sketch she had done of a 20-foot fountain of lights, the middle-of-the-yard centerpiece she and Alan wanted to create together – the glowing addition they were certain would lift them from a disappointing second place to glory in the city of Duluth's holiday lighting contest.

It was the crowning "wow" decoration that Alan never got the chance to build.

But Marcia still wanted to. With Shirley a constant comfort and companion, Marcia was finding a way to carry on. She was somehow finding a renewed determination, and she was reclaiming her zest for life – and for Christmas lights. If she couldn't decorate with Alan, she would decorate for him. She could finish what they started. She set out to win that contest. In Alan's memory.

But she needed help.

She took the drawing to one of Alan's oldest and dearest friends, a coworker of his and a fellow welder who, like her late husband, possessed skills and talent to turn a dream into a towering, metallic masterpiece.

After handing him the drawing, she waited before speaking, before asking. The anxious moments felt like hours.

"Is it possible? Can it be done? Or was Alan just kidding?" Marcia finally asked, the three questions all running into each other. After several more moments of hopeful nervousness, she spoke again. "So?"

Jolted from deep thought, Jim Anderson responded with a startling suddenness.

"Of course," he said, not taking his eyes off the picture. His mind raced with calculations and determinations. How can we pull this off? How can we put this together? And who was "we"? He had some immediate, pretty good ideas, and when he spoke again, it was with more confidence.

"Of course," he repeated, finally looking up, catching Marcia's hopeful gaze as it washed with gratitude. He returned it with a grin. "It's possible."

The project was launched.

Jim called on his son to help out, and he asked another of Alan's friends, a sheet-metal worker named George Jackson, to pitch in. The men jumped at the chance to sweat and to weld and to build together inside Jim's garage on the North Shore. They toiled for one special reason: to assure the legacy of a good friend.

"George and I worked on it two full days together. Then we had another full day of painting," Jim said. "We did it all for Alan and because Marcia asked us. He would have done it himself. I feel good that we were able to finish what he wanted."

Marcia motored up the North Shore daily to monitor the progress, to see for herself that the drawing and the dream really could become reality.

Both could – and did, one sweltering afternoon in late summer when the tower was delivered, in pieces that had to be assembled. About eight of Alan's former coworkers took up the task, erecting the masterpiece in a prominent corner of the yard, right where Marcia chose. With each level added, the structure soared above the grass and glistened in the sun. The tower of lights with the swooping circles at its base and the large star at the top soon was complete. And was magnificent.

With her deepest, most heartfelt thanks, Marcia offered payment. She insisted. "Please," she implored. The men refused, every one of them and every single time – without allowing even a single anxious moment to pass.

* * *

Out in her yard as often as possible – where she could breathe in Lake Superior, where the memories of Alan were as thick as mosquitoes in June and where his spirit lives as though one of the angels in the trees – Marcia seemed to all but forget she was running for re-election. That late summer and early fall of 1999, her mind tended to block out the reality that she was in a battle for her political life and for the opportunity to continue to represent 17,000 residents of Duluth's 3rd City Council District, roughly a fifth of the city's population. She was in a race against a formidable, contentious opponent, too.

44

"Four years ago, I ran and I said neighborhood voices must be heard," Marcia told voters. "I made a commitment to this community. The most important thing we do is listen to people in the neighborhood, and I have tried to do that."

But she was devoid of her usual energy in what, Marcia felt, became a very nasty campaign. She still cared – few would question that she cared as deeply as ever – but it was obvious her heart was elsewhere. In November, voters supported her opponent.

"I suffered two major losses this year," she lamented to a reporter. "I thought I was doing OK, but obviously it was difficult for me."

* * *

Marcia would run for election two more times – once in 2001 for an at-large city council seat and then the next year for state representative. After defeats both times, she doubts another run will be in her future, despite her desire to serve her communities and her strong political views. As she said to a reporter following one of the defeats: "I thank all my supporters. Tomorrow, I'm going to start hanging Christmas lights."

* * *

The first icy breezes of early winter howled off the big lake, battering at Marcia's small beach house – and battering at Marcia, too, her flimsy coat tossed over her narrow, hunched shoulders almost as an afterthought each time she stepped outside.

But it was done, ready for the contest judges. With help from friends, from her now-grown daughters, and from her small grandsons Zach and Foster, the decorations were complete. A fence of lights led from the back porch toward the beach. Eleven lighted archways formed a tunnel into the darkness. Lines of lights beautified even the highest branches of her towering blue spruce trees. Seven glowing deer shared yard space with a pair of penguins and a gaggle of Christmas geese. Mistletoe hung just above eye level. Icicle lights dangled from the roof lines of the main house and garden house. The large "NOEL" sign, spelled out with green rope lights, was back. So were shimmering white stars, bright snowflakes, and a lighted Santa flying from the treetops.

And at the center of it all was the commanding fountain, its brilliance a tribute to Alan, its 2,000 shimmering lights pushing Marcia's twinkle total to more than 40,000 bulbs, better than 10,000 more than she and Alan had the previous year.

Confident she had done all she could to impress the judges – and to honor her husband's memory – Marcia logged onto her computer, found the website for the city's annual lighting extravaganza, and entered, this year using her own name.

But then something strange happened. Nothing happened. Marcia didn't receive an e-mail acknowledging her entry. No one called to say they were coming out to judge and could she please make sure her lights were on by such-and-such a time and on such-and-such a date. No letter fell into her mailbox, alerting her that, sorry, but better luck next year. Nothing.

"I got a bad feeling," Marcia said. "I knew something was wrong. I called them, but I never heard anything back. They never contacted me."

The bad feeling knotted at the pit of Marcia's stomach the morning the contest's winners were announced.

The winners certainly were deserving; few could have argued the brilliance of their displays.

The residential division winner that year, for example, Jeannie Mosiniak, a postal encoding center employee, had spent the year drawing and painting characters onto sheets of plywood that her college-aged son, Bryan Anderson, then cut out and propped up in the yard. More than 50 characters – Santa, his reindeer, a gift train and baby Jesus, among them – greeted passersby enticed to slow down by the glow of 15,000 lights. "We've been adding to it every year, just like everyone does," Mosiniak said. "It started out with him helping me. Now I help him."

The Schaub family, as another example, took the masters division for previous winners by adding penguins and a beaver to their decorations and by highlighting their animated, rooftop deer and sleigh. "We like to be creative," Kathy Schaub said. "We like to give people something different to look at. It's hard work, but it's fun."

But what about Marcia? a *News Tribune* reporter asked at the awards ceremony, held once again in the posh reception room on the top floor of City Hall. The reporter was told Marcia hadn't entered. Pressing further, he later was told there had been a problem, a "computer glitch" that prevented nine brightly lit Duluth-area homes from being judged. Marcia's display was one of nine entries that had been lost.

Almost as disappointing as not being judged was not being listed among the brightest and best-decorated houses, as published that year in the twice-weekly *Duluth Budgeteer News* newspaper. Milt Hill, whose "White Magic" had won previously, was also one of the missed entries. "It's really bad news," said Hill, concerned that no one would visit his display. "I do this for others to enjoy."

Contest officials telephoned the missed decorators and apologized, profusely. They donated a small sum on behalf of each of the entrants to the Salvation Army and published an explanation in the next edition of the *Budgeteer News* that included the addresses.

Marcia was disappointed and "livid." The Special Honorable Mention hastily bestowed on her display did not assuage the anger, hurt or frustration heaped on top of a year of losses.

"This year was special," she said.

Or should have been.

from Marcia's Guest Book

I brought my sister here for her 16th birthday as a surprise. I had her cover her eyes all the way through Canal Park! I am broke, so this was my birthday surprise, so thank you for sharing it with us. I was here earlier in December with my girl friends. LOVE IT!

— Sara, Bayfield, Wisconsin 2005

We just got engaged here on the path to the beach. Thanks for the best spot of my life.

— Leah & Matt, 2007

MARCIA, WE'VE BEEN HERE 4 YEARS IN A ROW, YOU'VE BECOME A CHRISTMAS TRADITION FOR US,
— DIK LAPINE FAMILY (SUPERIOR)
PSALM 119:105

"WE THOUGHT WE SAW THE NORTHERN LIGHTS, BUT IT WAS JUST THE MARCIA HALE'S LIGHT DISPLAY."

10
Stories

After the disappointment at City Hall, Marcia went home. She petted Shirley. The dog jumped up, panted, and then bolted for the beach, leaving behind only a fuzzy, furry, gray blur. Shirley was adjusting well to her new home and had become the grand hostess of the lights, a role she would enjoy for many years.

Marcia found out that in addition to all her other challenges, Shirley needed to relieve herself frequently, probably because of her older age. But that was all right. Marcia was a homebody and could give the dog all the attention – and walks outside – she needed. Shirley was even getting along with Marcia's two cats, Mom, an orange-and-white tabby, and Howard, Mom's son. Except for one incident. Howard had sniffed at Shirley's food bowl, setting off a cartoon chase that didn't end with canned laugh. Instead, Howard was left cowering behind the clothes dryer until Marcia got there to help.

"After that they became very good friends, though," Marcia said. "Shirley just kind of fit right in. She knew her areas. She loved the beach and went to the beach every day. Whenever I was out doing the lights she came by me and kept me company. Good dog."

Marcia watched the dog go before heading inside and down to the basement where the breaker boxes were located. The late afternoon sun was fading and the sky was filling with crimsons and ambers. She hurried her step. She flipped the switches. Though she couldn't see it from where she stood, she knew her yard had just erupted with a glorious holiday glow. Returning upstairs, she flipped on her stove's burner so a giant vat of hot cider could resume its simmering.

She did all this, but really, would anyone have blamed her if she didn't? After all she had been through the past year – Alan's death, losing re-election, then being forgotten by City Hall and the contest judges? Would anyone have blamed her if she had simply left the light switch off and the cider unheated and the fire pit cold and quiet?

But Marcia didn't abandon her lights; never even considered it.

And at sundown, they came, like always, the "tourists." Marcia could almost hear Alan announcing their arrival. Like on any other night in December on Duluth's Park Point, they wandered through, gawked, marveled and felt warmer than they should have, bundled against subfreezing temperatures and frigid Lake Superior breezes. They huddled around the fire. Roasted marshmallows. Sang songs. Talked.

"It's so beautiful. I can't believe she'd allow total strangers to walk through her yard," said Duluth's Paula Zabinski, who shared the lights that year with her 4-year-old daughter, Sara. "But this is what the holidays are all about, isn't it, sharing with strangers?"

In the garden house, visitors signed Marcia's guest book. Over the years she would collect about 20 books filled with comments from holiday revelers and well-wishers from as nearby as down the street and as far away as Germany, Italy, Poland, Malaysia and Russia, or from exotic tropical locales such as Puerto Rico, the Philippines and Panama. Lights lovers from at least 20 different countries would leave messages. At least six couples would become engaged amid the glow.

The guest books themselves have become an attraction, Marcia said. "One woman sat out there and read from the Christmas books for about three hours."

People often leave a note about their gratitude for Marcia's welcoming place.

"Thank you for making my season. Your husband would be very proud," wrote one visitor.

"Winter wonderland. So perfect and sweet," wrote another.

"This is the high point of our holiday drive."

"Wonderful display. This is the true meaning of Christmas."

"Merry Christmas, Marcia. ... The (wishing) penguin brought us to Duluth – it's true!"

"Marcia, Al would be very proud of the work you have done. It is truly beautiful. I just want to say that Al is missed very much by myself and many others. ... I do miss him."

"We didn't plan tonight. This was such a blessing. I just got out of prison and my husband sent me pictures of this last year. This year I got to be here. Praise be to God! God bless y'all."

"We just got to town from Los Angeles to visit my mother. We saw the story about these lights in the newspaper and just had to come."

* * *

Asked about the guest book entries and the people who spend a few moments of their holidays on her property, within her creation, Marcia just grins as though she has a secret.

"Just having people come and enjoy the lights makes it festive. It's worth a million dollars to see the little kids' faces and the people of all ages who come here. I couldn't not do it. Holidays can be such a downer when you've lost someone. But you can't say, 'Well, I'm not going to celebrate Christmas this year.' You have to go on.

"Every light in my yard represents a new day. There are so many lights here. I hope they give people who need it one more small reason to go on."

Some nights, after everyone has left, after the drained cider vat has been taken back to the house and washed out, and after the lights have been turned off, Marcia sits in the garden house and reads the words scrawled in those guest books: the many reasons why people come, the ways some of them are going on in the face of difficulties. Marcia thinks about the stories. There are so many stories. And she realizes: The lights aren't about winning a contest. They aren't about out-decorating others. They're about what happens when people embrace them – the magic that transpires.

* * *

A woman stood at the edge of the brilliance one night, unable to bring herself to go in. She had lost her son that year; it was her first Christmas without him, she explained in halting sentences after Marcia approached to see if she was all right. Marcia stood with the woman as long silent minutes passed into another winter's night.

"Thank you," the woman said, finally. "Thank you for helping to ease my pain."

* * *

A young man came in a wheelchair pushed by a young woman. They had been there the year before, boyfriend and girlfriend. They had kissed under the mistletoe and had made promises. But that year he crashed his all-terrain vehicle while motoring along a wooded trail. He suffered a head injury. Though he could no longer remember his girlfriend or the life they once dreamed about, he could remember the lights, she said. So she brought him.

"That's the way life is, full of surprises," Marcia said. "Some good, some not so good."

* * *

It was a surprise to see one elderly gentleman as he arrived at the lights. He wore sunglasses and carried a long white cane, tipped red at the end. He didn't use it for support but to feel for the ground in front of him.

"I've been back three times," he told Marcia. "These are the most beautiful lights I have ever seen."

And yes, "seen" was the word he used.

* * *

"The stories keep coming," Marcia said. "They pile up year after year. It's hard for me to think about them sometimes – or to tell them – without choking up a bit."

* * *

Others tell stories, too.

Jessica Fabb grew up in Duluth, graduated from Duluth East High School in 1998, moved to London, wound up staying 6½ years while teaching kindergarten, married a Brit, had a son, decided Minnesota was a better place to raise children, moved back and lives now in the Twin Cities.

"My mom, sisters and I started going years ago, every Christmas Eve, and it became a family tradition. Some years, it was almost too cold to get out of the car, especially being a high schooler who was too cool to dress for the weather. I'd foolishly wear a skirt and tights.

"In 2008, I had come back to visit with my newborn son, Orson. It was a little early for her lights to be open to the public but we thought, 'Well, let's chance it and see if they are on,' as I had to fly back to London the next day. We got out and my mom, who is never shy, knocked on the door and told Marcia, 'My daughter is here from London and wants to see the lights.'

"I felt kind of embarrassed, but Marcia was extremely nice about it. She let us in from the cold and into her kitchen for a brief chit chat, and then she turned on all the lights that already were in place for us.

"We also went into the garden house and looked through her old guest books. We do that every time we see Marcia's lights. It is fun to see our signatures from over the years.

"Marcia's lights are so magical and we look forward to seeing them every year. We are so very lucky to have this here in Duluth!"

* * *

Another Duluth native, and a longtime student of Duluth history, Laurie Mattson, told this tale:

"I went down to her place one wintry night with a gal friend when I worked security at the EPA (the U.S. Environmental Protection Agency office in Duluth). I've told so many folks about the illuminated wonderland on the Point. Well, my friend, Ruth, was a computer genius, and when Marcia happened to mention she was having PC trouble, Ruth and I went inside her home and Ruth began trying to figure things out. Meanwhile, I kept her faithful pooch, Shirley, company. Marcia gave us cookies and tea.

"Just being with her gave us a sense of belonging. It truly was as if we'd known her for some time. I think Marcia is a gracious lady."

from Marcia's Guest Book

This is my 2nd time ever being here. We were in Canal Park and had to stop by. My family didn't believe me that this was here and wanted to turn around. Luckily they didn't! This place is so gorgeous! It's wonderful that you devote your time and energy to the spirit of Christmas. It makes the holiday season that much better. Well, Merry Christmas. See you next year! Thank you.

— Raeanna Wuorinen, 2003

Amazing!
– Hannah & André,
Sweden 2008

I can't tell you what a wonderful moment it was to share this magical spectacle with my 87-year-old mom who just regained her sight after laser surgery and cataract surgery this December. Talk about a sight for sore eyes!

– Gloria Walin
San Francisco, 2000

11

A Quarter a Day

There was a flash on the porch. Something reflected the afternoon sun, catching Marcia's eye. Curious, she shifted her grocery bags from one arm to the other and hurried from the garage to the house. Whatever it was, it wasn't very big, she concluded, mounting the porch steps. She saw it. Her eyebrows fell quizzically, furrowing her forehead.

It was a coin. A quarter. The way it was positioned, it didn't strike her as loose change accidentally dropped.

"What in the world? Did someone leave me a quarter? Who would do that?" Marcia wondered. "Weird."

And about to get weirder. Nearly every day she wasn't home that summer after Alan's death, she found a quarter waiting on her porch.

* * *

Jim Marshall was born and raised in Duluth's Lakeside. His mother, Mildred, was a court reporter who taught more than a few judges-to-be how to run a courtroom. His father, Rand, was a traveling salesman, selling dental supplies.

Jim followed in his father's footsteps, selling copy machines to life insurance to mining equipment to snowmobiles. He was the first Ski-Doo dealer in the United States, a venture that hit a snowdrift during the snowless winter of 1967-'68. He operated Chippewa Camping Outfitters on Miller Trunk Highway, equipping tourists for paddling trips to the Boundary Waters Canoe Area Wilderness north of Duluth.

He bought and ran what is now *Lake Superior Magazine*, publisher of this book, spotlighting the area's abundance of natural beauty at a time when smokestack industries were failing, jobs disappearing and the Duluth economy was as ugly as the area's lakes and forests were beautiful.

Jamar's departure from Canal Park may have signaled a change in Duluth from an economy dependent on heavy industry to one reliant largely on tourism, but it was cheerleading businesses like

Marshall's glossy and as-positive-as-he-was magazine that proudly helped ease along the transformation.

Jim was married and had three children. His wife, Beverly, died young when a blood vessel burst in her brain stem. She was 45. Jim remarried 15 years later, to Janice Biga.

Late in life, Jim – his hair as white as snow, still big in stature, boisterous in personality and his enthusiasm for Duluth as unwavering as a child's faith – embraced a desire to stay fit and be active. He bought a black Diamondback Schwinn with sturdy, wide tires, and he committed to riding the bicycle at least 1,000 miles annually. Most years he logged 1,200 to 1,400 miles, many of them from a building on Park Point near where he docked his 50-foot boat, *Skipper Sam II*, to Marcia's house and back. The ride was one of the flattest and smoothest the hillside city of Duluth could offer.

Jim had met Marcia through Alan, had tapped Alan's steel-fabrication skills to help him fix up his boat, had invited both Alan and Marcia out for rides on Lake Superior with Jan and him, and had been drawn to their Christmas lights with the same zeal he had for anything positive happening in the hometown he adored.

"Alan died on a Thursday. I remember that weekend Jim came riding up on his bicycle," Marcia recalled. "He just stood in the street with tears rolling down his cheeks. 'I can't believe Alan is gone,' he said. ... He made a point of riding here three or four times a week, at least, after that. And he'd always stop. I'd give him a Diet Coke and we'd just talk.

"We had politics in common; we were both conservative in our thinking," Marcia said. "Jim was always such an outgoing, positive guy. He told me once that when I ran for City Council I ran as a politician but after four years I had become a statesman. That meant a lot to me. 'I'm so proud of you,' he always said. 'You stuck your neck out.'

"It was fun to talk with him. He always treated me like an extended family member. He was quite the guy."

The admiration was mutual, insists Jim's daughter, Cindy Hayden, *Lake Superior Magazine's* publisher, a title she shares with her husband, Paul. The two have two sons.

"He admired Marcia. He liked when she was a councilor. And he really, really enjoyed the lights display. Biking down to Marcia's place was pretty much a daily goal," Cindy said. "I'm sure they talked politics, the city going to hell, that kind of stuff. My father was a pretty outspoken guy. They got along quite well. In Marcia and in Alan and in the lights, Dad saw Duluth's spirit."

In Alan, Jim also may have seen his son, Randy, who died years earlier of a heart attack. He was just 41. Like Alan, Randy was the type always happily willing to help. Also like Alan, Randy ran a steel shop. He was plant manager for North Star Steel.

"Al would grump at you once in a while, but he was outgoing mostly and smiling, glad to see you, glad to lend a hand," Cindy said. "His demeanor and personality and his can-do attitude were so much like Randy's."

Marcia didn't find out for months, until that following Christmas, that Jim was the one leaving quarters on her porch. She doesn't remember if he told her or if it was his friend Stan Salmi who sometimes rode with him who finally 'fessed up. And it didn't really matter.

"Just so you know I was here," Jim explained to Marcia. She smiled.

The daily bike rides continued for seven summers, highlighted by a Diet Coke if Marcia was home or a quarter on the porch if she wasn't.

But one summer the bike rides were no longer daily as Jim's health deteriorated. Early the following fall, Jim died of complications after a battle with Parkinson's disease. He was 75.

"The Northland lost one of its greatest promoters," the *News Tribune* eulogized.

"He was the consummate salesman," Earl Rogers, owner of Duluth Travel, told the newspaper after knowing Jim – or "J.R.," as he called him – for more than 40 years. "Whenever you saw him, he'd have a big smile on his face and out would go his big burly right hand."

"He was one of Duluth's big boosters," said Cindy. "He never thought of living anywhere but Duluth and he sure could have with his sales records. But this was his town and he loved it. Anything beautiful and positive in Duluth he was a cheerleader for – including the lights."

After Jim died, Marcia built a special display in her lights in his memory. Its centerpiece is a six-foot angel, its wings of brilliance outstretched. The angel is flanked by mirrors that reflect the rest of the lights in the yard and that glint, catching the eye. White pipes covered with more lights rise from the snow, their bases forming a half circle that starts at the angel and takes shape in either direction. The pipes meet 15 feet overhead, creating a sort of band-shell remembrance. Mistletoe hangs from the peak, decorated with pine boughs and holly.

Cindy and her family visit Marcia's lights every Christmas season, usually on Christmas Eve, just like they always did when her dad was alive. She spends extra time at the angel in the band shell now. She remembers, reflects, feels closer somehow.

And always, she leaves a quarter.

Just so you know I was here.

from Marcia's Guest Book

Our Christmas spirit is not fulfilled until we've come to visit you and Shirley. You warm our hearts with your wonderland of light and all of your giving.

> – Keleey, Joki and Jevin, 2003

This is just unbelievable beauty, some part of a fairy tale. You look and you can feel ... magic. Thank you very much for this feeling.

> *– Inna Cersick, Kevin Cersick, Kelly Cersick, Vitaliy H.*
> *Russia, 2006*

This was a very nice experience. ... We will definitely be telling others of this gem. Thank you very much!! Merry Christmas.

> *– Henry & Isabel Van Ramshorst*
> *Thunder Bay, Ontario 2008*

12
Pam

The last time Pam Limmer went out on a first date was at Marcia's lights. It was on a December 14, a square on the calendar now as important to her as even her birthday or anniversary.

She had met Dave at St. Luke's in Duluth where she worked as a nurse. He had been spending many hours there over several months, caring for a loved one, holding her hand during her final days.

When his loved one slept or was taken for tests, Dave talked to Pam. They shared a love of cars, they quickly realized. And motorcycles and road trips and adventures. Pam had just gotten a Ford Mustang convertible.

"That's it right there," she said, pointing out the window to the street below; the sports car shimmered in the sunlight.

She dug into her pocket and tossed Dave the keys. "Take it for a spin," she urged. Only after he left did the prick of potential foolishness strike her; she hardly knew the guy, even if it did feel as though they'd been acquainted all their lives.

But he returned. And after that she never was able to get rid of him – not that she wanted to.

After Dave stopped coming to the hospital, he e-mailed. For months. He told her about his job as a machinist in Superior at Barko Hydraulics and how he had been there 35 years. She shared hospital stories. They swapped tales of long motorcycle rides and seeing new and exotic places.

Eventually, Dave worked up enough nerve to ask Pam out. Eleven days before Christmas, he took her to Cloquet to see holiday lights there. Their date moved next to Duluth for dinner. Then they went out to see more lights, including Marcia's.

"I didn't know anything about Marcia or her lights then," Pam remembered. "We walked through and I remember thinking to myself, 'Man, this must take a ton of work.' We went into her little garden shed, and Santa was in there, so we talked to Santa. It was a gorgeous night.

"Had it been a year later, we probably would have sat on the beach. She has just such a gorgeous setting there on the water."

Had it been a year later, Pam probably would have whispered something more eloquent or life-changing into the ear of a plastic penguin she and Dave found about halfway up Marcia's tunnel of lights. Wearing curled-at-the-end ribbons of blue and green around its neck, the penguin stands next to a ground-level sign held in place in the snow by a wooden stake. "The legend of the penguin," the candy cane-colored sign reads. "If you make a wish while you pat my head, your wish will come true."

Pam patted and wished – to be happy. "Come on, it was just our first date," she said later, laughing.

But far from their last.

On December 14, 2007, Pam and Dave celebrated the one-year anniversary of their first date. Pam slipped on a favorite fuzzy-blue sweater vest decorated with stitched snowflakes and snowmen. She wore it over a long-sleeved sweater. Dave combed his mustache, pulled on a pair of jeans and positioned a newsboy cap over his close-shaved head.

The couple went to Grand Rapids for the day before stopping in Cloquet to see the lights there again. But Dave was "so dead set on getting home," Pam recalled. "He really wanted to [do everything] just like we had done the year before. He was nervous, but I didn't think anything of it. … I was starving. I wanted to eat."

"No," Dave said. "Let's go to Marcia's first."

This year, the couple took advantage of mistletoe they found in the lighted trees. They walked out onto the beach. And they spent time just soaking up the beauty and the holiday warmth. With awkwardness gone, they enjoyed just being together, even during long moments when neither of them felt the need to speak.

Santa was in the garden house, just like he had been the year before. Marcia's grandson, Zach, was there, too, snapping people's pictures.

"Your turn," Zach said to Pam.

"Oh, come on," he gently urged when Pam declined.

With a slight roll of the eyes and a smile that was all teeth and joy, Pam finally agreed, settling onto the Big Guy's bright red knee.

"Dave was on the other side," Pam recalled, "and before I knew it he was down on one knee."

And what in the name of all that's ugly was he holding? It looked to be made of rubber and was round and featured bright flashing lights. A ring, Pam finally realized. The gaudiest, most horrific ring she had ever seen. Yet when Dave held it out to her, she instinctively extended her hand. And she let him slip the bought-at-the-circus trinket onto her finger. He had been carrying the monstrosity around in his pocket for weeks – after literally buying it at the circus – waiting for just the right moment to give it to her, for just the right balance of humor and romance.

"Will you marry me?" he said.

"I didn't say anything for the longest time because all these people were watching," Pam recalled. "But then I did say yes. Of course I said yes. And I signed the guest book. I didn't tell anyone I was engaged, but when I went back to work, the woman in the pharmacy knew. She had been at Marcia's, too, and had read the book.

"That ring," Pam continued, laughing. "That was just the way he was. Very fun. That was so typical. I still have the picture of him putting it on my hand. It's in my dining room. The ring is on the table in front of it."

Pam and Dave got married, but not on December 14, which, of course, would have made this part of the story absolutely perfect. They married on October 3, in the middle of their backyard, choosing the same sort of setting Alan and Marcia had for their own wedding.

On December 14, they visited Marcia, though, bringing along plenty of photos.

"Marcia just opened her house and her heart and her arms to us," Pam recalled.

They promised to return every year. On their special day. To their special place.

The following December 14, Pam arrived at Marcia's without Dave. He had gone on a fishing trip to Crosslake, Minnesota, just 2¹/₂ months earlier, Pam explained, the words catching in her throat. It was the same annual trip he had been going on for 20 years. The same group of guys, too. One evening they were sitting around the campfire. The wind shifted; the smoke started to sting Dave's eyes. So he got up to move his chair. In the darkness, he stumbled over something. A rock, probably, or a piece of firewood. He fell, landing awkwardly on his side. He broke three ribs. His buddies rushed him to a small hospital not far away, but complications developed. They proved fatal.

"Such a waste," Pam said. "He was 58 years old. Had never been sick a day in his life. If he had had a heart attack or something, I could understand. This I couldn't understand. ... We bought a house together and never unpacked. We were never home. We went coast to coast in the three years we knew each other.

"I knew it was going to be really, really hard to go back to Marcia's. I took my son with me. I didn't want to go alone. But I definitely wanted to go," Pam said. "We talked a long time. And in the end I'm glad I went. I had to. Dave and I would have come together. It was our anniversary. It will always be our anniversary. As long as Marcia keeps decorating, I'll keep going. I'll go every year on our day."

To their special place.

I believe in angels,
   The kind that heaven sends,
I am surrounded by angels,
   But I call them friends.

– Author unknown

13
Ellie

Is there really magic – a special spirit – in Marcia's lights? Ellie was determined to find out.

The little girl limped with every step, but she managed to make her way up the path illuminated on all sides by twinkling, white-as-new-snow bulbs.

She had come with her mother and sister in the days leading up to Christmas. They had spent an hour or more marveling at Marcia's fountain of lights, at the fairies that glistened in the trees, and at the lighted polar bears skating on a small, frozen pond. They wondered how anyone could get lights into the tallest trees. And they gushed at the way the city lights, visible from the beach and from the path leading toward the beach, complemented, and even made more breathtaking, all the decorations.

Marcia noticed the family because she noted something peculiar. "As the other children tussled around, little Ellie sat quietly in a chair, just watching."

"Why are you sitting here? Why aren't you running around with the other children?" Marcia asked the girl who appeared to be about 4 but who actually was 9.

"I'm just tired," came the tiny response.

Only in the quietest and most private of moments did Ellie ever acknowledge the ailments that stunted her growth and hampered her development. Only to a select few did she ever admit to the pain that screamed from her underdeveloped feet and hips. Often, she just said she was "tired."

As tired as she was, Ellie determinedly traversed the illuminated path. One last time before heading home, she had decided. There was a little penguin in the tunnel. She had noticed it earlier. A little plastic penguin. The wishing penguin.

Dressed in a thigh-length, down-filled winter coat she buttoned all the way up to the red scarf her mom wrapped around her neck, Ellie paused at the penguin's feet before slowly, carefully, lowering herself to her knees. She bit her mitten, pulling it off with her teeth and extended her hand to pat the penguin on the head.

She had a wish. A Christmas wish.

And she believed in magic.

* * *

Ellie was adopted as a newborn by a Duluth couple who had adopted siblings about 10 years earlier. They adopted Ellie knowing she had a malfunctioning kidney that surgeons would have to remove. The surgeons wound up removing half of her other kidney, too, when Ellie continued to suffer fevers and other maladies.

When Ellie was 3, her adoptive mother, Lorene Olson, died of uterine cancer. She was just 44 years old.

Then, a month after the funeral, Ellie had to be rushed to the operating room at Duluth's Miller-Dwan Medical Center. Her face was filled with fear and uncertainty. Her eyes darted about the cold, sterile room, from one stranger to another.

"She had kind of a little, elf-like face," surgical technologist Toni Snickers recalled. "She reminded me of a favorite doll."

Toni smiled at the little girl, as warmly as she could, but the friendly gesture was returned only with an apprehensive silence, a penetrating gaze, and a stare "that just looked right through you," Toni said.

Ellie was in the operating room because she had suffered third-degree burns to her buttocks, ankles and feet. The injuries covered 15 percent of her body. Her teen-aged sister had been giving her a bath at home but had failed to check the water before putting her in. The burns were severe enough that grafts were needed to fix the damage. Some came from Ellie's back. Others had to be taken from her scalp, which meant shaving off her beautifully long, curly hair. Doctors used 200 staples. Ellie had to be anesthetized during the most difficult of the procedures.

"What a good kid she was, given what was happening to her," Toni recalled. "It was an accident, what happened. And she didn't complain. She didn't cry."

But Toni cried. That night when she got home, she broke down. She had a daughter of her own, Ivy, who was just a year younger than Ellie. She sat her own little girl down and made her promise. "Don't ever – *ever* – let anyone put you in a bathtub without checking the water first," she implored. "Please." Ivy promised.

Ellie recovered and eventually was able to go home to finish healing. Toni was left to wonder – and she did, "for a long time" – whatever became of the uncomplaining little girl with the penetrating gaze.

"There are just some patients you really remember," she said. And some you can never forget.

* * *

Three years passed. Toni received a phone call from an old school friend. Lowell Olson had been a middle linebacker at AlBrook High School. He graduated two years after her. She had been a cheerleader.

"I sort of had a crush on her in high school," Lowell admitted to Toni's sister, Jill Nyquist, a 1975 AlBrook grad, after running into her unexpectedly at a laundromat on Duluth's Central Entrance.

"[My sister] decided to play matchmaker," Toni said. "She told him that I moved back to Duluth a couple of years earlier after spending 20 years in Omaha.

"I was a single mom at that time, with Ivy. Her father passed away from a heart attack when I was three months pregnant. He was a mere 39 years old."

Toni and Lowell ended their phone conversation by exchanging e-mail addresses. They e-mailed for months. Finally, they decided to get together for a dinner date. Over appetizers and glasses of wine, they caught up.

Toni had returned to the Northland so her daughter could grow up closer to family, she explained. She told Lowell what it was like to work in the operating room at Miller-Dwan. There was heartache sometimes but also many days when you really felt you were making a difference.

Lowell talked about his job, too, how he had been working more than 20 years in internal sales for Motion Industries, a Duluth bearing manufacturer. He and his late wife, he said, had adopted three children, siblings first and then, about a decade later, a baby girl born with kidney disease and kidney malfunction. He lost his wife three years earlier to uterine cancer, he said.

"And then, about a month after that," he continued, "my poor little 3-year-old girl was scalded in the bathtub. ... That morning I was going to work and my daycare lady called and was sick. So my daughter, who had watched Ellie hundreds of times, and who easily was old enough, offered to stay with her."

Toni's ears perked up. The story sounded familiar. She shared her own story of a little girl she'd always remember, the little girl who also had been accidentally scalded in a bathtub and who she met in surgery.

The two froze, staring at each other. Could it be? Was it possible?

"Wait, I have pictures," Lowell said, leaning in his chair and reaching into his back pocket to produce his wallet. The rawhide flopped open and for a moment neither of them spoke. Or breathed.

"That's her," Toni managed, finally. "That's the girl I took care of, helping to remove her hundreds of skin staples.

"Her eyes," Toni remembered, unable to take her own off the photograph. Toni's face streaked with tears.

Lowell was dumfounded. "The coincidence was phenomenal," he said later. "So phenomenal. I had no idea she worked with Ellie in surgery. I couldn't believe it."

Toni and Lowell continued dating. How couldn't they after discovering the connection they shared? After about six months, they decided their young daughters should meet. Lowell's older children were grown by this time.

"Talk about two peas in a pod," Toni said of her Ivy and Lowell's Ellie. "They hit it off right off the bat, dancing and singing like girls do."

The girls hatched a scheme, also like girls do. Ellie doesn't have a mom and Ivy doesn't have a dad, they reasoned, sounding a bit like the long-separated twins in the "Parent Trap" movie. Life was imitating art.

"You could be my mom," Ellie said to Toni.

"And you could be my dad," Ivy said to Lowell.

Toni and Lowell became engaged soon afterward, were married, and began making trips to Marcia's lights as an annual part of their Christmas celebration.

"I felt that maybe, in some way, maybe there was a reason for everything that was happening," Toni said. "Maybe this child needed somebody. I really felt that this little girl needed a mom.

"I married Lowell because I love him but also because I love Ellie and I thought maybe I could be of some help to her. Ever since that moment, we've never been separated."

Including the year of Ellie's Christmas wish.

* * *

Not long after the wedding, Toni found herself noticing things about Ellie, starting with the way she walked. She limped and "she was listing to one side," Toni said. In addition, she suffered headaches and was wetting her bed. They took her to a doctor. And then to more doctors. A body scan and MRI revealed Ellie's hips weren't developing normally. Further exams showed her bladder was enlarged and her urethra was dilated. Yet another battery of tests indicated she needed to be seen immediately by a kidney specialist. The half kidney she had was only working at about 30 percent and was not producing the vitamin D or the iron her body needed for proper development.

"Now it was all making sense," Toni said.

* * *

Days before Christmas, her hand extended, Ellie paused, picking her words carefully. Then she patted the penguin on the head and whispered quietly, just to him: "I wish to not have any pain anymore."

That night, at bedtime, she reported to her mother her hips had stopped aching and that a headache from earlier in the day was gone. "I feel better now," she said.

* * *

The following spring a much larger ache was remedied when surgeons at St. Mary's Duluth Clinic realigned Ellie's hip socket by removing a piece of her femur and installing three screws and a plate. The operation was broadcast live on the Internet, making Ellie feel like a web star.

Two years after that, her medical metamorphosis reached its greatest heights – and its most critical moment – when Ellie, 11, was deemed eligible for a kidney transplant. While waiting for an organ to become available, she had to endure dialysis, stuck in her room for 12 hours every night, from 6 p.m. to 6 a.m. Outside, she could hear neighborhood kids squealing and laughing during the never-ending evenings of summer. But she endured; she persevered.

Ellie was among an estimated 70,000 people in the United States awaiting a life-saving kidney transplant that spring. That made her story one of tens of thousands of reminders of the critical need for everyone to register as an organ donor – and then to inform loved ones of the decision so there are no doubts or second-guessing.

Every time someone decides to become an organ donor, as many as eight lives can be saved, according to LifeCenter, an organ donor network based in Cincinnati. Pretty amazing.

True to character, Ellie didn't complain while on dialysis or after being admitted to the hospital for weeks of antibiotics to fend off a fever and stomach pain. Abba's "Super Trouper" wasn't only her favorite song, her family reported, it was her.

"It's not just about Ellie, though," Toni said during one of those many moments of anxious waiting for a life-saving organ. "It's about how important organs are and how important it is to check that box on your driver's license to become a donor. There are so many kids and adults who die every year waiting for an organ. And then there are those who throw their lives away. They really make me mad."

Fighting mad for just one more kidney, one more successful transplant, and one more person to make that decision to become an organ donor.

For one more angel.

* * *

At St. Mary's Children Hospital in Duluth, nursing assistants like Liz Severs care for hundreds of kids, most of them adorable, sweet and able to steal your heart.

But few like Ellie.

"She's, you know, she's her. She's Ellie. People who know her will know what I mean," said Liz, 24. "She came in smiling and laughing even though she was super sick. And, I don't know, we just clicked."

During Ellie's first 10 days in the hospital – 10 days of antibiotics and around-the-clock hospital care after being admitted with the stomachache and the fever of 100.5 – Ellie and Liz learned they shared a love for swimming, texting and the violin. Liz hadn't played in years. She gave her old instrument to Ellie. The two also tussled at Scrabble. Though only a sixth-grader at Morgan Park School, Ellie won the board game nearly every time they busted out the little square tiles.

"Because I'm the best at it," she teased.

Liz teased right back: "Oh, I let you win."

But it wasn't all games. During quiet moments, Ellie shared her story, the parts she was comfortable telling, at least. She was surprised how comfortable she felt with Liz, explaining how she needed a new kidney, a transplant that would save her life. She told her about the penguin and her Christmas wish.

Liz was surprised at how closely she was bonding with this patient. The more Ellie talked, the more deeply Liz was touched. She couldn't help but wonder whether she could help. Could I be a donor? She found herself asking.

"I went home and I researched it," Liz said. "As soon as I realized I could do it, I wanted to do it. It's hard to explain. I just knew."

Though she had known Ellie just six months, Liz took the incredibly selfless, unbelievably giving step of contacting the transplant center at the University of Minnesota Amplatz Children's Hospital to offer. The Twin Cities hospital gave her "reams of paperwork" to fill out. She underwent a medical evaluation, blood tests, and was asked to complete a 580-question personality test and psychological evaluation.

"It sometimes felt like they were trying to talk me out of it," said Liz. But they didn't. They couldn't. Liz wouldn't be deterred. This was what she wanted to do, needed to do. Her mind was made up.

Her family supported the decision. She grew up in a loving, close home in the far northern Minnesota city of Warroad, a windows-manufacturing, hockey-playing haven of fishing, hunting and camping. Liz's employers supported her decision, too. Both at the hospital and at a jewelry store in the mall where she also worked, her bosses were more than willing to let her take the time off she needed. Generosity continued, to Ellie's benefit.

"I do get nervous," Liz admitted in the weeks before the surgery. "But it's never, 'Oh, gosh, I can't do this.' "

For that, Ellie and her family were thankful beyond words.

"I keep thinking, every day, how incredible Liz is for doing this," Toni said at the time. "She's an angel. Our angel. It's amazing someone came forward who's so giving. Can you believe it? It is a miracle. What an amazing person."

Toni and Lowell kept loved ones updated on the transplant procedures via blog entries at caringbridge.org.

"Night before surgery," they wrote on Transplant Eve, which came just a few days after Christmas – and only a couple of weeks after the family's latest visit to Marcia's lights for cider and wishes. "We spent ALL day at the transplant center today, not only with Ellie, but also with our wonderful donor, Liz. They took 13 vials of blood from Ellie and 16 from Liz!!! Unreal. Surprised they both didn't pass out!!! I think we talked to everyone but the Easter Bunny and signed enough papers to get a new mortgage on the house! Ellie will be the first surgery in the morning. Which means we have to get up darn early – again.

"Hopefully, our story is and will continue to be on a happy note. Time will tell."

Toni and Lowell found far more to say the day of the transplant, the day Ellie and Liz "clicked" once again – "clicked" when it mattered most.

"Ellie was the first transplant this morning," they wrote. "Her amazing donor, Liz, went in first, at 7:30, then Ellie at 8:04.

"A little note about Liz. She is a self-proclaimed wimp! Yet she took it upon herself so do this fantastic feat! Unbelievable! (By the way the girls gave her a stuffed animal chicken mascot!)

"The surgery was a complete success. They both had post-op pain, but I will hold back on the language they spoke. I'm sure some of it had 4 letters! Liz's family were here and are wonderful people, as you could imagine.

"Visited Liz in her room … to say 'Thank you,' but what can you say? She responded, 'You're welcome,' as she drifted back to sleep.

"Still can't believe it. Still waiting for someone to wake me up. Tried to leave [Liz's] room without sobbing in front of her family but didn't go so well. Maybe they didn't notice?

"Anyone reading this, don't send us anything; please send it to Liz.

"So far, everything is going well."

* * *

Ellie and her family were able to leave the hospital after about a month of recovery – and a month in the Ronald McDonald House. They returned to Duluth, the proud recipients of a fully functioning kidney, and when Ellie went back to Morgan Park Middle School, she was welcomed like the returning hero she was. She was able to go swimming again and be with her friends. She even went to a dance. Rarely was she seen without her trademark smile or her infectious energy. She was her usual bubbly self, friends reported.

"Life for Ellie has been pretty darn good," her family said at the Caring Bridge site.

But during one of Duluth's most pleasant springtimes – including the only snow-free March in the city's recorded history – Ellie started "not feeling all that well," her father posted.

"I kept an eye on her vitals," Lowell wrote. "Toni took the day off of work … to bring her in for a throat culture, as she complained about a sore throat. The results came back that she had strep. So they did send her home with amoxicillin to take for the next 10 days. … I went online this morning to get the results [of recent blood tests], and everything looked good and in order."

The report was concerning, but not alarming. Strep throat typically isn't anything serious, anything to worry about. And "good and in order" on the lab work: Those are always positive words.

But, Lowell continued, "They added another test, which was a test for mononucleosis. [It] came back positive. Yikes. I immediately contacted Ellie's transplant coordinator to see if there were any additional drugs that she needed to take. We did get a response back to change some of the nighttime and daytime doses to see if this would do the trick. So I guess from here we just wait to see how these drug changes and the amoxicillin help her out in the next upcoming days. Right now she is very stuffed up and congested with a very sore throat. No school or swimming for her for the next couple of days. Hopefully everything will work out and things will get back to normal again. ... Let's just keep our fingers crossed for now that she can overcome this bout with illness to go on as a normal child."

There seemed no reason to think she couldn't. Or wouldn't. She always had. No one who knew her could imagine a barrier her courage and determination couldn't bash through.

Toni took more time off from work to stay home with Ellie. Her doctor in Duluth prescribed Tylenol with codeine. Administering the medicine required rigid, critical scheduling.

"She was miserable," Toni said. "I woke right at 4:30 and felt the need to check on her. When I did, I lay my hand on her forehead and it was cool. At first I thought, 'Good. Her fever broke.'"

But then Toni noticed something. Bubbles on Ellie's lips. Her heart sank. Her knees buckled. She knew.

"Ellie! Ellie!" she screamed. But there was no response. Lowell woke up and immediately dialed 911.

"I picked up her little body and put her on the floor and started to administer CPR," Toni said, "trying to bring life back into our baby."

Toni continued compressions until paramedics arrived. They took up the effort.

"I could not save her," Toni said in the days that followed the little girl's death. "Lowell kept hoping, thinking that (the paramedics) would bring her back. ... We barely got to the ER when the doctor came back and told us she had passed on.

"Ellie had lived through so much: kidney taken shortly after birth, burns, hip surgery, dialysis, transplant. She fought so much. And then to die in our home over strep and mono?

"I know Ellie is with the Lord, and Jesus took her out of her pain. I know that. I know we did the best we knew how. Yet it does not make it any better right now. We always knew that Ellie had a long road, but we never imagined this. (We were) always positive – like her. Everyone who knew her loved Ellie. She touched so many hearts."

Toni and Lowell ended the Caring Bridge entry with a message to their little girl: "May your spirit live on in all of us, our most precious peanut."

Early the next morning, Lowell logged onto the computer again to share the terrible news. He wrote that "she passed peacefully and is now in the Lord's hands."

After enduring so much, after teaching the rest of us how to be brave in the face of insurmountable challenges and how valuable life is – so valuable we should never stop fighting for it – after all this, one of the bravest, strongest little girls ever died. She was just 12 years old.

* * *

Santa gave Ellie a stuffed penguin the year after her wish. "She makes me feel better," Ellie said of the toy, which she named Penguina, and which she slept with every night.

"I wished upon the penguin," she said. "And I think that my wish came true. Because I believed."

The guest books Marcia puts in her garden house are filled with wishes people believe were granted by the wishing penguin. An unexpected job change allowed one family to move to Duluth after they made that wish, they wrote. Others shared stories of wedding proposals, long-dreamed-about babies and more.

But Ellie's story, Marcia said, is the most remarkable. Ellie wished to "not have any pain anymore." Her wish was granted.

* * *

"Ellie has suffered more than we can imagine. But unlike some of my coworkers, who can come up with anything to say they are suffering, Ellie rarely complains," Toni remarked that year. "She endures. The rest of us can learn from her, and we can forget all the problems we complain about that aren't really that big."

Ellie's family never missed a Christmastime visit to Marcia's lights. The year after Ellie's Christmas wish, and after surgeons realigned her hips, Ellie ran through the decorations. Again and again. Just like the other kids. Marcia watched and marveled. She vowed never to forget.

from Marcia's Guest Book

*This was a great place to come to during finals week.
Great study break! Thanks for the cider!!*

> *– University of Wisconsin-Superior
> Women's Hockey Team, 2007*

**Thank you for the spirit of
Christmas. I really needed this.**
–Deb from Omaha, 2003

*Thank you for reminding us about the magic and
selflessness of Christmas. I'm almost 60, and your
lights and displays brings us both back to around age
10. 'Tis a cold night to walk around with one's
mouth wide open, but certainly well worth it. Thank
you so much, and do have a blessed Christmas.*

> *– Paul & Anita Helbach
> Brule, Wisconsin, 2005*

**God bless you and thank you. My
inner child thanks you as well.**

> **– Ellen from Cloquet, 2003**

14
Follow the Cats

The crusty, frozen, trampled snow scrunched under Marcia's boots. She carried a bucket of sand and a small shovel. A scoop at a time, she sprinkled the paths beneath her lights to give visitors traction. The sky was a deepening purple. The bright blues and faint pinks of an hour earlier were now hugging only the horizon.

The first cars were arriving.

"Hello. Welcome," Marcia called to her first visitors of the evening. Three slow-moving, elderly women, each wearing a stocking cap, mittens and an overstuffed coat that hung down near their knees, climbed out of their car. Puffs of fur stuck up from the tops of their boots. They were ready for the elements.

"Shirley will show you around," Marcia joked, gesturing toward her bearded collie. Shirley wore little red booties on her feet and a red sweater pulled over her head and around her midsection to protect her, too, from the frigid Duluth winter. She loved the many visitors, and the visitors loved to pet and nuzzle her.

"Or you can follow the cats," Marcia continued, grinning, noticing that Mom and Howard also had come outside. It was the same tongue-in-cheek advice she offered to so many lights lovers, especially the first-timers.

"What?" The ladies were skeptical and grew more skeptical when Shirley darted off in one direction and Mom and Howard started up the path into the yard in a completely different direction. Follow them?

Others came and Marcia soon forgot all about the three women. Eventually, Marcia made her way to the fire pit, which by then needed a fresh log. About to toss on another piece of pine, she suddenly paused. She heard, coming from the neighboring property, a rustling and a crunching of fallen tree branches. It would have sounded like a deer coming through the woods if not for the irritated voices. Marcia couldn't quite make out what the voices were saying.

Then she saw them. The three women. Approaching from the dunes and the beach beyond. They were stomping through a portion of the neighbor's yard purposely left natural and with undergrowth to hold back sandstorms. Mom and Howard broke into the yard first. Were the women dutifully following Marcia's four-legged feline family?

"I didn't mean ..." Marcia started when the women also re-entered her decorated yard. Then she turned to hide her laughter. "Oh, my," she said just to herself, laughing some more.

The women looked bewildered and stone-faced. Their stocking caps were askew. Their mittens and the fur poking from the tops of their boots were covered with burs.

Marcia turned back to them. "Sometimes the cats don't stay on the paths," she apologized. She invited the women into her home to warm up.

from Marcia's Guest Book

We are first-time visitors of your light display, and we had a wonderful walk through the winter wonderland and look forward to coming back soon. Thank you for sharing your love and passion with us. We took some pictures to share with the rest of our family in Norway. Thanks again and happy holidays!

— Kristin & Mike Thornburg
Trondheim, Norway, 2003

We have traveled four years to Duluth and what we talk about most to everyone back home is your beautiful light display. No one does it any better. Thank you!!!!

— Gary and Lori Schneekloth
Bellevue, Nebraska, 2006

We love that Santa landed on the beaches of (Lake) Superior to bring us this!

— Kati, Kelli, Grant, Gretchen Wirkkula, 2003

15
Finnish Tradition

Every year when the biting, swirling winds of autumn become
the stinging, icy gusts of winter, and around that time when turkey,
pumpkins and Thanksgiving give way to thoughts of nog, holly and
Christmas, attentions across Duluth turn to one thing.

Ice candles: hollowed-out blocks of ice with candles inside,
producing a heavenly glow.

Okay, not everyone's attention, but enough Duluthians have
been inspired by Marcia to create fire-and-ice works of illumination
art like hers that the city could lay claim, if it ever really wanted to,
as an ice-candle capital. How about the Ice Candle Capital of the
U.S.?

The Ice Candle Capital of the World – or at least of Canada, a
country with a high enough frequency of frostiness to allow such a
thing – has to be the tiny hamlet of Kenora, about a two-hour drive
along the Trans Canada Highway east of Winnipeg, or about three
hours straight north on Highway 71 from International Falls,
Minnesota. On Christmas Eve every year, as part of Kenora's
Festival of Lights, 50 volunteers light 5,000 to 6,000 ice candles in
the city cemetery in memory of loved ones lost.

Marcia makes about 25 ice candles in her yard every year. They
mark and light the paths for visitors.

Do-it-yourself books, craft shows and websites galore offer tips
and instructions about how to make the luminaries, but few result
in creations as large as the ones Marcia figured out how to make
through trial and error many long winters ago. Not that her
technique came easily.

The first year she tried to make the frozen candle holders all
she did was freeze blocks of ice.

"And then there I was on Christmas Eve, out there with a drill
trying to drill holes into these blocks of ice. It didn't work. I didn't

get the effect I wanted," she said. "Not at all." The ice walls were so thick the glow of the candle could hardly be seen.

The next year a friend suggested placing an empty bucket inside a bucket filled with water and then putting them both outside to freeze. The result, the friend fathomed, would be thinner, more illuminating walls. But that didn't work, either.

"The buckets twisted and didn't come out right," Marcia said. "But I kept trying. And finally I figured it out."

She figured out that if she filled squarish, four-gallon kitty litter buckets with water and then allowed them to freeze for a while, but not for too long, she could tip the buckets over, pour hot water over them to separate ice from plastic and drain out ice melt as well as water that never had a chance to harden, leaving behind a perfect cavity for a lit candle. Perfect because the walls of the candle holder are thick enough not to melt anytime soon from the heat of the candle inside but thin enough so the glow of the candle can be seen from the outside.

"I remember telling people one night it's an old Finnish tradition, that Finnish people on Christmas Eve put ice candles on the graves of loved ones," Marcia said – and she was actually absolutely correct. The tradition can be traced back centuries to the European nation.

"But I'm not Finnish," Marcia continued. "I was so quick to say that. I made such a point of that. I don't know why. There's nothing wrong with it, with being Finnish. Well, the people looked at me and finally they said, 'Well, we're Finnish.' There was this huge moment of embarrassed silence, then we all had a big laugh."

Lee Campbell told a newspaper reporter one Christmas season that she had been making ice candles, and had been carrying on the tradition from the Old Country, for 10 years – ever since visiting Marcia's.

"I saw she had these odd-shaped, square ice candles. They were beautiful, just huge," said Campbell, who is from Duluth's Norton Park neighborhood. "She just had the candles in the blocks of ice. It's taken me 10 years of experimenting, but I think I improved on her idea with the decorations."

Yep, decorations. Campbell started using pine boughs, pine cones and other natural accents as well as tinsel, ornaments and other Christmas favorites to dress up the insides of her ice candles. She started giving the candles as gifts – just not under anyone's tree in the living room where they'd surely melt and make a huge mess.

She also started using the candles in tribute to her father, Ray Campbell, who's buried in Duluth's Forest Hill Cemetery.

"An ice candle looks lovely in a dark cemetery on Christmas Eve," Campbell confirmed. "It casts a beautiful light and is a special, enchanting display."

And that's true whether you're Finnish or not.

from Marcia's Guest Book

It warms my heart to know there are people like you who share their creativity and hospitality for all people who come here. You are the shining light in Duluth in more ways than one. Thank you. May the holidays thoroughly delight you.

– Sue Fortien, 2003

This is so unique and incredible. It's so neat to see people doing such fun things for anyone and everyone to come and enjoy. We will definitely be back again. Thank you!

– Aaron & Stacy
P.S. Shirley is adorable, 2003

What a wonderful place; it's like walking through the night sky.

– Marnie Wolowich, Scott Chanook
Thunder Bay, Ontario, 2005

The note from Shirley is very touching. This is my 3rd year here and that note brings tears to my eyes every time. Thanks for touching my heart. Shirley!

– Kim Bernachki, 2006

16
Shirley's Angels

Shirley quickly became Marcia's much-loved and much-needed constant companion.

Almost every day in summer, Marcia would trek along the sandy beach outside her house with Shirley beside her. So would Mom.

"We sort of looked liked a Disney family," Marcia laughed. "Mom cat and Shirley and I would walk the beach.

"That first summer, there was a straw hat out in the lake," Marcia recalled. "Shirley swam out there and brought this hat back. I went and got a camera. 'Okay Shirley,' I said, 'pose.' And she did pose with the straw hat on."

Sometimes after their walks, Mom and Shirley would just curl up together.

Though Marcia considered Shirley "older," she found herself constantly pestered to play catch with the enthusiastic pooch. Finally, one day after about six months, Marcia felt overwhelmed by the constant throw-and-fetch, throw-and-fetch.

"Enough!" she declared.

Shirley calmly stopped the game and sat down, as if she'd wondered all along when enough would be "enough."

Marcia was amazed – and relieved. And the next time she saw Carrie, Shirley's former owner, she had questions. The first: Why didn't you tell me about the 'enough' command? "Oh," Carrie responded innocently, "didn't I tell you about that?"

Shirley knew lots of tricks – sit up, lie down, beg – and gladly performed for anyone. "It was like, 'I'm on show. I'm going out there. I'm going to do my tricks,'" Marcia said.

Shirley even received a movie offer. Sort of. In 1993, when Carrie had been working with the dog trainers for the Disney

85

movie "Iron Will," filmed in and around Duluth, they urged her to take Shirley to Hollywood. Or to let them take her.

"She was so animated and smart and trainable," Carrie said. "You could think about a trick, and she was already doing it."

"Beardies are that way," Marcia said. "Beardies are very, very smart."

Like other bearded collies, Shirley's mop of fur needed continual care. Marcia groomed her and also brought her to a woman in Duluth's eastern Lakeside neighborhood who sometimes had to shear the dog almost like a sheep.

Marcia felt blessed to stumble upon a dog who offered such great comfort and who had such a welcoming personality.

"Shirley just loved everybody," Marcia said. "She was thrilled to see people."

* * *

Her last Christmas, Shirley didn't go outside much. She didn't lead visitors through the lights or playfully drop her ball at their feet, panting and looking up expectantly until they picked up and tossed the slobbered orb for her to retrieve. She was old. Tired. She spent most of her time wandering about the house or curled up in her favorite easy chair in the living room. She was content.

But one night Shirley suddenly bolted from her chair and made a beeline for the back door. With a loud "ARF!" she stood on her hind legs and pawed at the wood, catching Marcia's attention.

"What in the world?" Marcia asked. She had come in to check on another vat of cider and to warm up a bit. Lots of people on this night.

"Well, Shirley, look at you. My goodness," Marcia said, walking toward the graying dog. "What is it?"

She opened the door and Shirley bolted out like she hadn't in years. As fast as her geriatric legs could carry her (which actually wasn't very fast), she lumbered toward the garden house. Marcia watched her, then grabbed a coat, tossed it over her shoulders and followed.

Two steps out of the house, Marcia heard it, too.

Singing.

"What in the world?" she whispered.

* * *

They came to Superior from all over the country, from all sorts of backgrounds and life experiences. They came to study music at the University of Wisconsin branch located in Duluth's twin city. They attended many of the same classes and nearly all of them sang in the same college choir.

"We were a pretty tight-knit group," said Rachel Vanda of the northern Wisconsin city of Spooner, about an hour south of Superior. "We went for fun."

The young students went as a group to see Marcia's lights because they needed some fun. Final exams had finally finished, releasing a valve of stress and anxiety so strong it launched them with too much energy into their Christmas breaks.

"My mother told me about the lights. She said how magical they were, and I just had to get out there to see," Rachel reported. "I invited a few friends."

Seven co-eds in all, they walked through the lights. Then walked through again. Then they lingered, the way so many before them had and so many have since.

"We were just enchanted," Rachel said. "The lights were so beautiful. And the night was so beautiful."

"We have to sing a song," one of them suddenly suggested.

"You think?" questioned another. "No one else is singing."

And then they just did. Like a flock of birds that suddenly and inexplicably changes direction mid-flight, the group harmonized and made music together with just their voices.

"We just started singing," Rachel said. "Without really thinking about it. We just wanted to. It just felt so right and it just happened."

"Joy to the World" was first: "Let e-e-very-y hear-hear-heart prepare-are hi-im roo-oo-oom. And heaven and na-ture sing. A-and heaven and na-ture sing. A-and hea-e-ven and-heav-ev-en and na-ture sing."

More carols followed before the group took the impromptu concert into the garden house and out of the cold. Nearly everyone there that night crowded inside to hear.

The admirers included, finally, Marcia and Shirley. The old dog clambered clumsily inside, glanced around and howled with the singers before snuggling up next to one of them, a young lady shorter than the others, a young lady named Shannon who, somehow stood out despite her lack of physical presence.

"What a sweet dog," Shannon commented between carols, slipping off her mitten to scratch Shirley behind the ears.

To thunderous applause, the group from the University of Wisconsin-Superior sang "Silent Night" and "We Wish You a Merry Christmas" before taking bows and enjoying well-deserved sugar cookies and Styrofoam cups filled with steaming cider.

"Oh, that was just marvelous," Marcia gushed. "And look at Shirley. She doesn't get like this for anyone anymore. You sound like angels. I got tingles and shivers listening to you."

Rachel, Shannon and the others thanked Marcia for her kind words. Then they offered a few of their own: "I think God is working through us to bring you a touch of the joy and magic and mystery of the season that you give to everyone else every year with your lights and yard," Rachel said. "You bless us with warmth and love and friendship. We thank *you*."

"You're an angel choir," Marcia announced, noticing how Shirley wanted so badly to be part of their magic and beauty. "You're Shirley's Angel Choir."

"Shirley's Angel Choir," the students repeated. The nickname sounded good. It sounded right.

They headed outside to pose for a picture in front of the castle of lights. Its brilliance glowed from the inky darkness of the moonless Lake Superior behind it.

Shannon gave Shirley a final pat and rub before they all left. The old dog nuzzled her in return.

* * *

The summer that followed was hot. Beastly by Duluth standards. Unbearable compared to the norm of Park Point, where cool breezes always seemed to be blowing in off Lake Superior, even in summertime – especially in summertime. Nowhere is Duluth's moniker as the "Air Conditioned City" more apparent than on the sandbar neighborhood.

Shirley spent most of that summer in the house, curled up in her favorite easy chair with the windows open and two fans blowing on her. Whenever she could muster it, though, she got up to play catch – still her favorite game. "She always had the puppy in her," Marcia said. "You never saw her limping; you never saw her laying in the dirt."

Until those last days. Marcia kept tabs on the dog, growing more concerned and then more sad with each passing day. Shirley was old – 17. Most bearded collies lived to about 12. Her fur was becoming matted, her demeanor listless and her eyes less lively.

One morning, Marcia rubbed Shirley's head and scratched her behind the ears. Lethargic, Shirley barely responded.

"She deserves more dignity than this," Marcia decided.

She grabbed the cordless phone and dialed Carrie. The city's animal control officer, and Shirley's previous owner, could bring a needle, Marcia knew. She could bring the dignified ending the dog deserved.

"You should bring Ryan, too," Marcia urged. "He'll want to say goodbye."

Carrie brought her red-eyed son. She also brought two needles. But upon arriving she stuffed one of the needles back into her bag. There would be no reason to tranquilize the dog to take to a veterinarian's office, she realized. Shirley wasn't about to protest. She perhaps couldn't.

"It's time," Carrie agreed, looking up at Marcia. They both nodded knowingly. Agreement didn't make any easier what they needed to do.

"Today you're doing it for Shirley," Carrie consoled and reassured, trying to ease the pain and sadness she saw in Marcia's eyes and that she knew was reflected in her own. "Had you waited, you would be doing it for yourself. This is right."

"I know," Marcia said, stroking the dog's fur, saying her last goodbyes. "I feel I owe this to her."

Marcia's four-legged constant companion had helped her through some of the darkest days of her life following Alan's death and had become as much a fixture among her lights as the penguins or campfire or guest books.

"I'll never forget you," Marcia said, kissing the dog on the top of the head.

Carrie motioned, and Ryan cuddled in behind the dog – his dog, too, his dog first. He wrapped his arms around her one final time. He held tight. And he spoke softly, nuzzling his nose behind her ear.

The needle found a vein. Shirley didn't flinch.

"The word euthanasia means 'good death,' and if anyone went in a good way Shirley did," Carrie said. "I remember how crazy busy she was when she lived with us in the hillside. Here, there and everywhere she would run. And we'll always be able to remember the trips we took with her to Iowa, Florida, Washington state and California. She lived for going places with us. We really loved Shirley a lot. She was quite the dog, a wild thing.

"And she was in heaven when she was here at the lights playing hostess."

"Everyone knew Shirley," Marcia chimed in. "Lots of people would come to the Christmas lights and say, 'Oh, we know Shirley,' and it wasn't from having been at the lights before, either."

"Everyone *loved* Shirley," said Ryan, who grew up to be a hospital corpsman in the Navy after graduating Wrenshall High School.

"She especially loved kids," said Marcia.

"And she was smart. You could talk to her like she was human and she'd understand," said Carrie.

"I don't think Shirley knew she was a dog," Ryan laughed. "I don't think it occurred to her she wasn't a person."

* * *

Few humans have raised as much money for a good cause as Shirley. Every year in the garden house, Marcia places a can with a picture of the bearded collie and the words "SHIRLEY'S FUND" on the outside. Night after night visitors stuff the can to overflowing with dollar bills, fives, tens, twenties and sometimes even larger bills. Marcia has never kept any of the cash, not even to help pay for cider. Instead, the money – all of it, about $1,200 to $1,300 a year and nearly $13,000 in all – has gone to Duluth's animal shelter and the Duluth Animal Benefit Fund. The money helps care for homeless dogs and cats, and it paid for a spay-and-neuter program in Duluth. Contributions to Shirley's Fund even provided seed money to help build a new animal shelter on the outskirts of the city.

Marcia's ongoing fund and annual donation to the city and its forgotten felines and canines always has shown her "deep love of animals and her 'can-do' attitude," as Animal Allies Humane Society then-president Cher Franzen once wrote in a letter published in the newspaper. Marcia, Franzen stated, was always "willing to do whatever it took" to benefit animals and always was "willing to go that extra mile."

"She was constantly looking at ways to help our cause for the many animals we serve," Franzen wrote. "[Marcia] has an understanding of the basic values Duluthians live by, and her priority is to support the needs of Duluth."

* * *

Fittingly, it was Ryan who gently carried Shirley's body into Marcia's backyard that hot summer day. About halfway between the memorial to Alan and the spot where Marcia and Alan once exchanged vows, Ryan dug a final resting place from the sandy soil. He carefully lowered the dog into it and then scooped dirt back on top. He planted a blue spruce over the place.

A marker was added later in front of the spruce, paying tribute not only to Shirley but also to a dog named Comet, who used to visit the lights with a boy who lived a few doors down Minnesota Avenue. The two – boy and dog – would sit for hours in the garden house, Marcia recalled, the boy writing notes that he left behind about how beautiful the lights were and how he wished he could live there forever. The boy and his family had recently moved to the neighborhood and perhaps, Marcia speculated, he didn't yet have many friends.

"SHIRLEY, the mystical Beardie," the marker read. "She loved everyone and everyone loved her. She was a legend. This tree is dedicated to Shirley, her friend Comet, and all the other pets who have gone on to the rainbow bridge. They lit up our lives."

At the edge of the yard, Marcia put up another marker, a memorial, this one featuring a picture of Shirley in her red booties and red sweater. "Shirley is no longer with us," it reads, "but her spirit will happily guide you through the lights."

Even if not always along the designated paths.

* * *

Some years Marcia could spot "Shirley's Angel Choir" practically before the co-eds hit her property. Their visits became an annual tradition. Always they opened with "Joy to the World" and always they finished in the garden house with "Silent Night" and "We Wish You a Merry Christmas." Always, too, they posed for a group photo. One year it was with Santa. Other years they smiled and shouted "Cheese!" under an archway of lights or elsewhere where they most strongly felt the soft glow of the holidays.

"It just feels so joyous to be there and to sing there," choir member Rachel Vanda said. "It's just wonderful to come back year after year and to sing again and again while enjoying the lights. All of us together."

The group's ranks have changed some over the years. Underclassmen have been invited to join the tradition. Some have brought along new boyfriends or girlfriends to join the angelic refrains. And older students have graduated, not all of them returning year after year for a night many of the others wouldn't dream of missing: their night of music and camaraderie in a place that embodies the spirit of Christmas, that just feels right.

"One year a woman was there. She had lost a loved one," Rachel recalled. "We didn't know it. She was just standing there like everyone else. But she talked to a friend of ours. And our friend told us later that when we sang "Silent Night" it really meant a lot to her. She told our friend she felt soothed and relieved from that, from hearing us. That made us feel so good. You never know the impact you can have."

One year Marcia didn't recognize the group. It was the year Shannon wasn't with them, and Shirley wasn't around to notice.

Shannon was the "charismatic" one of the bunch, Rachel said. "You remembered her. She was always upbeat and strong-spirited. She had an incredible sense of humor, a sarcastic, witty dry sense of humor. And always she had a great outlook on life."

All of which masked the reality that she was legally blind, had been born without a hip, hadn't grown normally and had endured a life filled with pain, surgeries and uncertainty.

"It was hard for her to walk. It hurt. But you would never know," Rachel said. "She was always the one perky and upbeat and always giving her love."

Until she couldn't anymore. She died just after Easter, slipping away in her sleep.

"I think her body just couldn't take anymore," Rachel said. "Medications and things were keeping her going at the end. And she was always pushing herself. She never stopped. She was so active. How did she do it? How did she keep going like that?"

Those who sang with Shannon at Marcia's and who attended music classes with her at the University of Wisconsin-Superior were embarrassed to realize they didn't even know how old she was. She grew up in Colorado and had relatives there and in California. They knew that. But was she in her late 20s? Early 30s? Probably somewhere in there. And just what was it that drew her all the way to northwestern Wisconsin for college?

Everyone always assumes they'll have time to ask such questions of a friend, that there will always be another chance to get to know someone better. But there isn't always more time, there isn't always another opportunity.

Shannon's family held her funeral back West. Her friends in Minnesota and Wisconsin weren't able to participate, weren't able to get together to grieve – until the next Christmas season when they made their annual pilgrimage to the backyard display on the shores of Lake Superior. Inside a gazebo strung with lights, and around a sign that read, simply, "IMAGINE," they lit a candle, they held hands, and they shared stories of their friend, the heart and lifeblood of their group.

"I talked about the strength of her spirit and how she always shared her love and joy with us," Rachel recalled. "Others mentioned her sense of humor."

After a long and lingering moment of silence in tribute to the newest angel now forever remembered at Marcia's lights, the group slipped into the garden house. They sang "Silent Night," just like they always did – and yet not at all like they always did.

They still come, year after year, always jazzed up at having just finished finals, always ready to sing and to become, once again, "Shirley's Angel Choir." Rachel and another young woman pick the date and send the word via e-mail or Facebook or word of mouth to students still cramming for finals and to graduates near and far. They make their plans. They keep the tradition alive.

"It's been beautiful. We love the lights, and we love Marcia," said Rachel, now graduated herself and living in Duluth where she teaches piano, directs musical performances and plays organ for churches.

"Marcia has the most beautiful place to sing carols in all of Duluth. What could be more fun than singing carols while surrounded by enchanted lights?"

from Marcia's Guest Book

Thanks for the gracious hospitality. I'm from New England and have never experienced this ... really wonderful ... thanks for the memory.

– Peter C.
Providence, Rhode Island, 2003

Thank you for bringing the Christmas spirit to life and sharing it. The lights and the waves bring me home for the holiday. You share so much by sharing the lights and the generosity. Merry Christmas. God bless.

– Aubrey Gold
Oregon City, Oregon, 2005

It just keeps getting better!
– Todd Lindahl & the Olsons
from Two Harbors, 2003

Marcia:
Thank you so much for the pleasure of your lights.

–Jim Averitt & Mikki Salzmann
Ironwood, Michigan, 2005

17

A True Winner

One more time, for one more year, Marcia paid a December visit to Duluth City Hall. She pulled into the circular Priley Drive, the brick-paved, tree-shaded lane named for the St. Louis County commissioner whose gardening skills turned from drab to dazzling the Civic Center courtyard and whose holiday lights Marcia's family always made a point of visiting when she was a girl.

She searched for a place to park in the shadows of buildings with their own rich past. The Duluth Civic Center's jail, federal building, county courthouse and city hall were constructed between 1909 and 1928 of stately granite and marble carved with ornate details. Lions' heads stand guard over doorways. Roman pillars hold up arched windows. The buildings were placed – together in 1986 – on the National Register of Historic Places. Laid out in a U-shape and given an unmistakable air of strength, power and authority, the Civic Center was designed by celebrated American architect Daniel Burnham, the same Daniel Burnham who popularized neoclassical architecture in the early 20th century with his "White City," the centerpiece of the 1892 World's Fair in Chicago, and the same Daniel Burnham who led America's City Beautiful Movement in the early 1900s. The Civic Center remains one of the movement's premier and best-preserved examples. It's a national treasure.

Marcia nosed her car into an open space, plugged the meter, headed inside and through the portrait-filled Hall of Mayors. She pressed "4" inside the elevator.

Room 405, the Mayor's Reception Room, greeted her with its familiar opulence. She paused to take in the view. She never tired of it, remembering it well from her many evenings spent exactly one floor below in the City Council chambers. Large picture windows accented with swooping drapery framed the scene: Duluth's iconic Aerial Lift Bridge, the busy harbor behind it and Marcia's Park

Point neighborhood beyond that, stretching out into the distance, seemingly all the way to the north woods of Wisconsin on the horizon.

Beneath one of the room's six glass chandeliers, each as fancy as in any ballroom, Marcia found a seat among the overstuffed sofas and high-back chairs that lined the walls. Upright chairs, some covered with lush red leather, surrounded, at the center of the room, a 20-foot wooden table, stained dark like the walls and polished to a high sheen.

The table dominated the room just as a pair of paintings dominated the end walls. One was done in 1893 and was called "Leif Erikson Discovers America." It had once hung in the lobby of what was, in its day, one of Duluth's ritziest hotels, the downtown Spalding, a 19th-century, turret-cornered, grand brownstone. The painting of the Norse explorer navigating rough seas had been donated to the city by the S.L. Washburn Estate and by the Lake Superior Region of the World League of Norsemen. The other painting, by Kipp Soldwedel, depicted a tall ship named the *Christian Radich* going out from the Duluth ship canal in 1976.

Would this be the evening that Marcia's ship would come in?

More people poured into the reception room for the announcement of the winners of the 2000 city of Duluth holiday lighting contest. One after another, her fellow decorators, city officials, community leaders, even media members and others greeted Marcia. They reassured her and they offered their encouragement because they knew her story; they knew all about Alan and the overlooked entry of a year earlier.

Marcia waited anxiously while other winners were announced.

The commercial division went for the second straight year to West Duluth's Lake Superior Zoo. Ten zoo employees had toiled more than 100 hours to run 3,000 feet of extension cords, coordinate 12 outdoor electrical timers and string 25,000 to 30,000 mini lights. The display, free for the community to enjoy during special evening hours, also included lighted polar bears, reindeer, a flamingo, snake, frog and gecko. There also was a Christmas star, bell and wreath.

Fourth place in the residential division that year went to James and Joyce Makowsky, whose story was one Marcia appreciated. James Makowsky was an avid collector of Coca-Cola memorabilia, and he built a lighted Coke truck for the family's display on West 10th Street. But the rest of the decorations had to be put up by the couple's grown children. They hurried home from North Dakota and the city of Virginia, Minnesota, to do just that. "My husband had open-heart-surgery this summer and I'm disabled so we called the kids," Joyce Makowsky told a reporter there for the announcement. "We said, 'If you want the stuff out, you've got to come help.'" The Makowsky kids wanted it out – for their father and mother, to give them a bright and cheery Christmas. They gladly came to help.

The residential division's third-place prize went to Eric and Deb Madson of Proctor, a small town nestled into the highlands just beyond western Duluth. Their centerpiece was a nativity scene.

Second place was won by Don and Pat Lowinski of Rice Lake Township, another community on Duluth's outskirts. Two years earlier, on a frigid December day, the Lowinskis' garage and nearly all their holiday decorations had been destroyed in a fire. "We couldn't decorate at all ... and we really missed it," Pat Lowinski said, explaining why even second place meant so much. "It was so dreary." In 2000, the family rebounded, buying new decorations and piping music outside. The rooftop was the highlight, covered with a Santa, a snowman, and a Christmas tree, all decorations that had survived the fire two years earlier.

Marcia shifted in her seat. Only first place was left in the residential division. This was it.

But when Mark and Debbie Glazer were announced as the winners, an audible gasp could be heard in the reception room. Not that the Glazers didn't deserve the prize – or their neighborhood, the well-lit Exhibition Drive, a hilltop street long a favorite among the Duluth region's slow-driving, light-loving, Christmas-reveling crowd. Some even compared the street to the bright lights of Las Vegas.

"We all enjoy putting up lights and we did enter the contest as a neighborhood," Debbie Glazer explained. "We didn't realize there wasn't a neighborhood category. The best part is that people enjoy it."

But what about Marcia? Had she been forgotten ... again?

The contest officials remained at the podium, however, beaming and bringing out one last trophy. It was made of bronze and was the day's largest.

"The winner in the masters' division," came the announcement, "is Marcia Hales of 3739 Minnesota Avenue."

The masters' division normally was set aside for past champions, but that Marcia should have been a past champion was enough.

Throughout the awards presentation, there had been polite clapping for each of the winners. But as Marcia made her way to the front of the room, the applause was thunderous, nearly deafening.

"I tried harder than I ever have," Marcia said, and she wasn't kidding. She added an amazing 20,000 lights to the 40,000 she already had. She also spent hours in her basement, stringing lights onto the frames of numerous new deer. Additional plastic penguins were placed around the yard. Sugar plum fairies filled dark spots in the trees. And a large lighted castle, at the top of the tunnel of lights and at the crest of the sand dunes, gave the display yet another focal point.

Marcia said she didn't want to talk anymore about what happened the year before.

"That's in the past," she said, reaching for the trophy. "This is for Alan. ... Maybe this win was a year late in coming, but that's all right. It's still special to me."

from Marcia's Guest Book

THANKS – better than Rockefeller Center!
– Katherine Gutierrez and Kevin Hinds
Queens, New York City, 2007

*You put our southern hospitality to shame!
Thanks for warming our hearts.*
– Lorie Hodges
Thomasville, Georgia, 2006

Well, I must say that I thought us Brits go overboard and are very festive but I think that you have beaten all of the British at their own game. The cider was very nice. Thanks.

– Stuart Bell
Birmingham, Great Britain, 2003

*Martha Stewart would be jealous. It is
a wonderful display.*
– Natty Wollack
Chicago, Illinois, 2001

18
Golden Standard

Marcia took home the masters' division trophy again in 2001 … and in 2002, and every year after that until she had collected eight of the coveted bronze beauties.

In 2008, the contest people pretty much threw up their hands as if to say, "Look, Marcia, your lights are as good as it gets; how about letting someone else hoist the hardware?"

They gave her a new honor, a Gold Standard Award, "for the lighting standard set for all of Duluth."

Marcia happily accepted and stepped aside from the city lighting contest. It had been years since decorating was about winning anyway. She came to realize that over many Christmas seasons.

"The lights are about what happens when people come to see them. It's about the giving and sharing of friendships. It's awesome. I love people, so it's a fun thing to be able to do," Marcia said. "These lights aren't about me anymore. And they aren't about winning anything anymore. I'm fine."

The lights are as much a part of Marcia's life as they've become embedded into the Christmas traditions of growing legions of annual visitors. Those who come year after year have been able to marvel at the display's spectacular growth and the way it changes in both subtle and not-so-subtle ways. It's no wonder they keep coming back – and telling their friends.

In 2001, Marcia put out 45,000 lights – "and a unicorn, Cinderella carriage and two snowflake trees," as the *News Tribune* reported, before teasing: "As if a castle, sugar plum fairies and deer weren't enough." One of her penguins held an American flag.

"The meter is spinning," Marcia joked that year, referring to her electrical meter. She never complained about power bills, though, and she certainly never accepted contributions to offset any costs.

"I don't talk about money," she told a woman shooting a documentary. "I consider this a gift to the community, and I never tell anyone what I pay for gifts."

In an interview with the *News Tribune*, she acknowledged that, "It does add up," but also that, "It always seems to work out."

It worked out – or Marcia made it work out – year after year, from 6 to 10 p.m. weekdays and until 11 p.m. weekends in the weeks leading up to and a couple weeks beyond Christmas.

Visitors came to marvel at the lights, to stop at the garden house for hot cider, popcorn and cookies. Some slipped donations into Shirley's Fund for the animal shelter.

And Marcia continued to grow the display, often to remember those missing from the pathways.

In 2002, she added a breathtaking new decoration, a swan that stood five feet tall and measured four feet across. Marcia made it out of rope lights and positioned it at the top of the tunnel of lights, to the left, just before the path that veers toward the beach. The swan was a memorial to Susie Ramsay, the young woman Marcia replaced behind the counter at Continental Ski Shop way back in 1964. Susie, who left to open her own business on the downtown Skywalk, died in November 2002 after a three-year battle with cancer.

"It's nice to have (the swan) there as a memory," said Susie's big sister and Marcia's good friend Jeanne Koneczny; they grew up together in West Duluth, where everyone just seems to know everyone else and easily become life-long friends.

"My brother, when he came from California, we went down there together," Jeanne said. "I still go every year. My husband will do the fire pit and roast marshmallows. I'm thankful it is there. It's really nice – and nice of her to do."

A major home-improvement project threatened to derail Marcia's lights in 2003. She invested more than $40,000 to replace her roof, add new windows, put up maintenance-free vinyl siding and remodel inside. She replaced her old fuse box with circuit breakers, a nod to her growing display's growing thirst for power. And she snaked trenches through her yard so wires could be buried and outlets added at various key locations.

If Rudy the exchange student ever visited again, Marcia figured, he could use the microwave to warm up a cup of coffee or just about anything else without fear of throwing the neighborhood into darkness.

Despite the ongoing home-improvement work, the display –
now 50,000 green and white bulbs strong with eight-foot lollipops,
an igloo for the penguins and striped candy canes decorating the
posts along the tunnel of lights – opened to the public as usual that
November, somehow without a hitch.

The lights grew to 75,000 bulbs in 2004 when the display
featured also a star fairy, a snowflake fairy, a flamingo, a seahorse
and a 24-foot, 3,500-light swirl tree. Santa returned to the garden
house on the weekends and Marcia put up for the first time a board
on which visitors could leave photos for others to see and enjoy.

The swirl tree was a memorial to John Young, Duluth's city
assessor from 1984 until his retirement in 1992. In 1997, he won a
coin toss for an interim position on the City Council. He died in
2003 after a short battle with cancer. He was 73. "His greatest
accomplishment on the council was passing a resolution requiring
the council to say the Pledge of Allegiance at the beginning of the
meetings," Marcia recalled of her longtime friend.

Additions a year after that included three skating bears, 15
miniature twinkle trees and another 15,000 or so light bulbs,
pushing the total to about 90,000. Was there anyone at Menards
who didn't get giddy at the sight of Marcia pulling into the lot?

"It's fun," Marcia told the *News Tribune* that year, estimating
that about 40,000 people were visiting annually. That's about 800
to 850 guests – or "tourists" – a night. That's a lot of cider.

"It's turned into a tradition for so many people. There are so
many stories," Marcia said. "I call it Duluth's original walk-through
light display."

Marcia marked a decade of serious decorating in 2008, the
same year she received her Gold Standard Award. That standard
stands at better than 120,000 lights now. She often gets a
decorating hand from her grandson, Zach.

"It's a magical place," *Duluth Budgeteer News* Editor Jana
Peterson once wrote, with "lights outlining a castle, a cascading
fountain, fairies that hide in the trees and more – and background
music provided by the crashing of the waves on the shore of Lake
Superior just over the dunes."

"Her lights are fantastic, just fantastic," added Marcia's mother,
Virginia Nyquist, who still lives in the warm, working-class house
in West Duluth where Marcia grew up. "The whole family goes
down there every year to see them. We always make a point of
going down there. Nowadays, the stores have come out with
everything you can buy. That doesn't turn me on. Marcia does all

the work – and has done it practically all alone since Alan is gone. I have to hand it to her, climbing those trees and everything. She makes Christmas – and not just on Christmas."

In 2009, Marcia was asked to help judge the city lighting contest. She eagerly accepted. And she offered to host the awards ceremony in her yard.

"There is some kind of spirit here," she said. "I can't explain it to you. It's magic; it truly is."

from Marcia's Guest Book

**Thank you so much for this display.
It is so heartwarming to see people
still this blessed with the Christmas
spirit. I love you for this!**

> **– Emily Fulton
> Duluth, 2003**

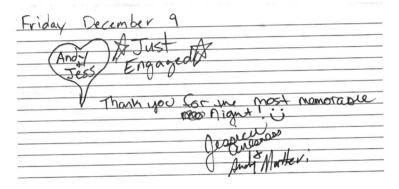

*Such a feeling of Christmas!
Thanks for bringing us extra joy today.*

> *– The Bush Family
> Chicago, 1999*

*Was so unexpected to come across this;
made it a magic night for two old foggies!
Thank you.*

> *– Unsigned, 2003*

19

Beyond Christmas

The Christmas lights weren't even on – not in the middle of summer. Still, as the sun started to set on a windy, cool evening, a true Park Point evening, Marcia's ears perked up at the familiar cruuuuunching sound of gravel under tires outside. Her eyes found the window and she realized a car – no, make that two cars – were approaching.

"I'm sitting here in my house," she recalled, a hint of a grin forming at the corner of her mouth, "and I see these people pull up, and they get their picnic basket out and they walk through the arches."

The arches that lead into her lighting display stay up year-round now. Dismantling and packing away the largest of the decorations wouldn't be practical. And really, where would she store it all?

Marcia hurried outside. "Hello," she called after the group.

"Hello. We hope you don't mind if we have a picnic in your park here," one of them responded, as friendly and as innocently as a dinner guest requesting just a bit more wine.

Park? Marcia thought. Picnic? "Umm …"

Finally, with classic Marcia graciousness – and frankness – she answered: "I guess it doesn't matter; feel free."

And they did feel free. They stayed hours, eating their macaroni and other treats. When they decided to light a fire in the fire pit, Marcia hurried out with the hose. "In case the fire gets away from you," she said as the wind continued whipping in off Lake Superior.

She went back inside but couldn't help keeping tabs on her "guests." Finally, she approached them. What's their deal, she wondered? She found an extremely friendly, enthusiastic bunch who didn't find anything strange at all about their choice of picnic locations. They invited Marcia to sit beside her own fire.

"Then we started to talk and they stayed for about another hour," Marcia recalled.

The evening finally ended and the two carloads of visitors headed out, the sound of crunching gravel chasing them down the driveway and out to the road.

Three weeks later the same two cars returned.

Marcia and her grandson Zach were in the yard. A beautiful, bright Saturday afternoon, the sort Duluthians really learn to appreciate while enduring so much snow and bitter cold. They were stacking wood near the fire pit. Never too early in Duluth to get ready for winter.

"Need help?" Without waiting for a reply the visitors helped move the wood pile. They stayed and visited again and Marcia found herself laughing and joking, as if with lifelong friends.

"They'll stop kind of at random now," she said. "I never know when."

"We try to stop by as often as we can; we just do it spur of the moment," said Julie Haberle, who leads the treks to Marcia's from her family's home in the Twin Cities suburb of Minnetonka, Minnesota, about 2$^1/_2$ hours south of Duluth, or from her family's cabin on Chub Lake, not far from Cloquet, 30 miles west. She runs a ministry centered on the debate over creation and evolution. Her husband, Paul, is a contractor.

"Heck, we'd hang out (at Marcia's) all the time if we could," she said. "She's just so darn interesting. For some reason we really hit it off. We can not see each other for a year and then go there and it's just delightful. We've brought tons of friends there. We just love her to death. She's just like family."

That's how it has become with lots of folks. No matter what time of year it is, Christmastime visitors return to Marcia's, to her yard and to the hospitality of a friend who always has coffee on, even if it's for acquaintances she has scarcely met. They pop in, often just to say hi.

"I like that, actually. I enjoy that. I'm never alone then," Marcia confided. "It doesn't bother me. I just sort of take it for granted, this place. Once they meet me it's like they're my best friends forever. That's nice, really."

The regulars include Donna Kennedy, when the pain allows, who showed up on that wintery night coming home from seeing the hand surgeon in the Twin Cities. She always has her camera. In the summer, she sometimes comes on her motorcycle. Like so many others, Marcia said, "I never know when she's going to stop."

No matter who's there, the conversation, inevitably, turns to the lights, the common denominator, the flame amidst the moths. "I hope you're doing the lights again," Marcia hears time and again, all year long.

"I don't think it would work real good to just say, 'No, I can't do the lights.' It's become a tradition," she said. "When you look in the guest books, you see the families that come year after year."

While others might tire of the upkeep and the costs related to keeping the tens of thousands of lights lit, and while some might be turned off by strangers who drop in unannounced – even in the middle of summer for a picnic – that just isn't Marcia. Or the spirit of her lights, which, apparently don't even need to be turned on for others to be drawn by their glow.

from Marcia's Guest Book

It is our first time experiencing your beautiful winter wonderland. Thank you for bringing about Holiday cheer! Merry Christmas and Happy Holidays

> – Nicole Alton and John Knoll
> Fargo, North Dakota, 2007

Thank you. This is really great. I'm a UMD student & I spent my first Christmas away from home last year and just happened upon this place on Christmas Eve. It really made the night special.

> *– Sara Palmer*
> *Williston N.D., 2003*

Much thanks to you. My daughter was 12 hrs. from home this year, and she came out to your display – much to my delight – there is a home away from home. Happy holidays.

> *– Janet Palmer*
> *Williston, N.D., 2003*

20

In the Light

Across Minnesota Avenue and on the other side of the harbor, the sun was still high above the Blatnik Bridge. The sky remained a pale blue. Marcia had at least an hour or hour and a half before full-on darkness and before the first of her final visitors of the season would arrive. Christmas had been celebrated more than two weeks earlier, but the Serbian Christmas was only a few days past. The Serbian Orthodox Church uses the Julian calendar and this was the first weekend after the Serbians' January 7 Christmas Day. And the weekend every year Marcia calls it quits for another season of lighting.

Her boots made a "p'foomp" sound as she broke through crusty, weeks-old snow on her way to the penguins and igloo. "P'foomp, p'foomp, p'foomp." One of the critters had tumbled in the wind and needed to be put upright. "There we go," Marcia said, wiggling his feet into the snow until they found solid support. She repacked snow around. She checked the wishing penguin. He stood tall, proud and ready to be patted, ready to continue the magic.

The temperature had been dropping all afternoon and stood in the single digits. Marcia wondered how many would arrive for the final night. Puffs of warmth gathered momentarily around her face before being swept away angrily by gusts off the icy lake. The smoke from chimneys all over town bent sideways, leaning to the south, conceding defeat to the nasty northern winds.

The campfire had to be started. On her way to the pit, she paused, momentarily, as she passed by the memorial to Alan.

"The way I deal with loss is to throw myself into a project," she once told a television reporter. "Getting into the lights just gave me a new sense of hope and focus.

"I'm always amazed at people that come from other parts of the country who go, 'Holy cow, I can't believe somebody would open their house,' and, 'It was a leap of faith.' But I guess it was, really."

A leap she never regrets. A leap that changed her life, gave it a new focus and purpose and opened her up to new people and unexpected rewards; those personal awards are always more satisfying than any award that's won.

At the fire pit, Marcia paused again, her eyes searching the treetops for a shooting star she made with pure-white rope lights. The star, with lingering trail, is a tribute to Ellie – and is about the size Ellie was when she died. A deserved memorial. An undeserved loss. On the ground in front the stand of pines that hold up the shooting star, Marcia positioned a simple sign: "Shining so bright and gone too soon," it reads in red, all-capital letters. Marcia couldn't help but read the words for the thousandth time, remembering Ellie and remembering a comet she once saw streaking over Lake Superior before burning out prematurely.

"Ellie sort of was like a shooting star," Marcia once reflected. "She was very bright and vibrant and hopeful and then, before we knew it, she just wasn't here anymore."

Turning her attention back to the fire pit, Marcia patted together a bed of twigs, small branches and newspaper pages. She set in a few larger logs and then stood three planks up on end, leaning them against each other. She pulled a match from her coat pocket and struck it.

The glow from the fire, faint in the evening's earliest hints of darkness, illuminated nearby decorations. The ones closest to the ground would be removed and stored away by spring. If they weren't, squirrels and chipmunks, invited to Marcia's yard with handfuls of peanuts, would gnaw at the wires, ruining them.

Marcia replaces all of the lights every two years. All 120,000-plus of them. They burn out. Entire lines stop working. Her green bulbs fade until they're clear, eliminating her accent color.

"It's a lot of maintenance," she acknowledged. "It's kind of like a job." A job she loves, even if it means having to be home and to stay home after about 3:30 p.m. every day – every single day – from the Friday after Thanksgiving, all through December and well into January, year after year. And even if it means sometimes spending Christmas alone while her own family gathers at her mother's house.

In the fall, when she brings back out the ground displays and finishes replacing what needs to be replaced, is when Marcia adds lights and new decorations and more of her unique creations. "Even this year," she said two Christmas seasons after receiving the city's Gold Standard Award, "I designed two new fairies and did a lot more out on the dunes. There are thousands of new lights out there."

The fire roaring, Marcia hurried down several steps she built one summer by half burying native bluestones. She made her way toward the garden house. Her coat hung open in spite of the frigid cold. Her stocking cap had gotten into her eyes and had been taken off and forgotten somewhere. Other things demanded attention. The shadows were getting longer. Time was running short.

Inside the garden house, about the size of a photo studio, Marcia stepped past her bronze trophies and the row of wooden Santas her mother had carved by hand decades earlier. News clippings, collected and framed over the years, hung from the walls. Marcia made sure the cider was still hot and simmering, that the ladle was at the ready, that her latest guest book was opened to a fresh page, that the donation can for Shirley's Fund was at its most eye-catching position, and that the lights that ran around the room, up near the ceiling, were turned on and working. Check, check, check, check and check.

She crossed to the house and headed into the basement. In an instant – and without the dramatic, sparks-flying boom that switches always make when flipped in movies – Marcia's yard simply and silently just filled with light. Glorious light. Breathtaking light. A brilliant warmth of holiday magic and cheer.

"It's the spirit of the season," Marcia said, taking it in, a look of utter satisfaction washing over her. "It's hard to say the lights are about loss. But they do give comfort to people who have lost. It was my way of grieving that first year after I lost Alan, to keep my attention on a goal and to keep busy.

"God willing my health will hold and I can continue doing it. I'm fine. I don't need a lot of help. And I realize a lot of people make this a tradition. It is expected. They look forward to it and I love doing it. So I'll keep doing it.

"I call it my winter gardening. People say it's magical. It does have that kind of ambiance, with the fairies and angels and everything."

* * *

"One reason I call it 'holiday spirit in the lights,'" Marcia explained, "is because there seems to be some sort of spirit that people get when they step into those lights. I can't really even describe it … it's peaceful. There's just the Mannheim Steamroller music, but it's not loud and blaring. It's the ambiance of being by the lake and with the trees. It's sort of a spirit of community, too –

where you have big people and little people. I can remember nights where people have reunited who haven't seen each other for years. People come from CHUM (the Churches United in Ministry shelter). They really don't have a place to have Christmas. They're homeless. There's just a broad variety of people who come. I've never heard an angry word."

* * *

Drawn, the visitors arrived. One last time. One last night.

A pair of women first. A mother and daughter? Sisters? There was really no way to tell. Their coats were zipped over their chins; their hats and hoods were pulled low over their eyes. They walked through slowly, made their way to the beach, returned, and warmed up at the fire pit before finding Marcia. She was tinkering with an uncooperative decoration, not far from the angel memorial to Jim Marshall.

"Thank you for putting on the lights," one of the women called.

"Oh, you're welcome."

"What a beautiful view from the beach," said the other woman, clumsily adjusting her stocking cap with hands that were covered by oversized choppers. "There are all your lights and then the city lights down the beach. I saw those and said, 'Wow, Marcia really did a good job!'"

"I do try," Marcia responded, laughing.

"Yeah, you did it up," the first woman jumped back in. "Thank you for having it. This is the best."

A man approached next. He wore no hat and only a thin fleece jacket. He couldn't have been from Duluth, or even Minnesota. Locals know better than to venture out like that.

"Thank you so much," he said, explaining he was from Memphis, Tennessee, and had just been driving by. "I saw how beautiful this was and I just had to stop."

"I'm glad you did," Marcia said. "What are you doing up here?"

"Business," he said. "You know, I just love your lights. I hope people let you know how much they appreciate it."

"Oh, they do," said Marcia.

Another woman, as well bundled as the first two, joined the conversation. "I love that almost all the lights are white," she said. "It just gives a serenity to the whole scene."

The woman's eyes followed the lights toward the heavens, which were starting to fill with stars. "How do you get the lights way up high in the trees?" she asked.

"I climb the trees," Marcia answered to the delight and the chuckles of her visitors. "I do. OK, I also have a big ladder my husband bought me one year and I have these long poles that I use."

"Oh my goodness," one of them marveled.

"Good for you."

"It's actually kind of nice in October when we have a nice day," Marcia insisted.

"Will you keep on doing this?"

"Oh, yeah, you bet," she said, her accent and generosity still classic northern Minnesotan.

"This is just lovely," the praise continued.

"Thank you," Marcia replied again and again. "Thank you."

from Marcia's Guest Book

Blessed be! This is a marvel most joyous.

— Unsigned, 2003

21
My Story

Everyone in the family seems to recall it differently, that year we discovered the wishing penguin. We all made wishes – but there is only one that we all still remember.

We had been coming, together, to Marcia Hales' lights ever since I was assigned to write a story about them and about Marcia for the *News Tribune*. The story was fun, and I quickly created a mini-beat for myself that allowed me to tell tales each December of lighting and of area decorators and even of decorating trends. I also took over compiling the newspaper's annual list of brightest and best houses, knowing the list of addresses, a longtime tradition for Duluth, found its way onto the front seats of limos, senior center buses and countless family vehicles. I reveled in helping people have a brighter and merrier Christmas.

The wishing penguin, my family and I learned years later, was the invention of a 4-year-old girl who wrapped her arms around one of the many plastic penguins in Marcia's yard. Why she picked the one she picked no one knows. Her Grandma, a friend of Marcia's, made sure the little girl's wishes – usually for whatever was the gotta-have-it toy that year – came true. "Maybe," Grandma joked in the *News Tribune*, "the penguin has the powers of opening the pocketbook."

The penguin came to belong to everyone the year Marcia placed the sign in front of it, promising wishes whispered to the penguin would be granted.

My own 4-year-old, Charleigh, believed it the year we first noticed the penguin. She crouched down. She rubbed the critter's head with determination. She patted it hard. Then she rubbed it again just to be sure.

On the way home she announced, "I'm going to get a new baby sister. I wished on the penguin and I'm going to have a new baby sister."

"Oh, brother," her big sister, Claire, sighed.

Julie and I just looked at each other. We had long dreamed of being blessed with a third baby. But it had been years since our last child and we were now pushing our 40s. Our time had passed, we figured.

"Maybe Santa will bring you a doll," we offered.

Charleigh wouldn't hear it.

She knew what she asked for and she trusted what she was told, that the penguin granted wishes.

And doggone if it didn't. Two months later, while treating ourselves to leftover cake from Charleigh's fifth birthday, Julie and I were privileged to break the thrilling news: We were indeed going to have another baby.

"And it's going to be a girl," Charleigh shrieked.

Doggone if it wasn't. Regine was born that fall.

Before long, she, too, was told all about the wishing penguin and was begging to go see it, to go whisper into its ear.

When she was 3, she didn't even care that it wasn't Christmas anymore or that spring was fast approaching.

I was working on this book at the time; maybe I was talking about the penguin; maybe that was why she suddenly needed so badly to go visit.

"The lights won't be on," I told her.

She wasn't fazed. Off we went.

I knocked on Marcia's door. A regular visitor those days because of book work, I explained we were just running up into the yard for a second.

We had a flashlight. We would be fine. We'd be quick. We did not, I teased, have a picnic basket with us.

Reggie got to the penguin first. But before she could pat it or rub its head or whisper in its ear, the yard around us erupted in a warm and dazzling glow.

Marcia had run down to the basement to make sure our visit, even if it was just a quick one, was memorable and special.

So like her.

"Go ahead," I said to Reggie, who was wide-eyed with wonder at the lights everywhere. "Make your wish."

Finally, she did.

She patted the penguin on the head. Three quick raps with the palm of her open hand. Then she straightened up, took a step back and put both hands on her hips.

"Well," she said, "where is it?"

"It's not like a vending machine," I told her, smiling. I scooped her up into my arms, looking into her chocolate-brown eyes, just like mine.

"Wishes do come true, though," I said, giving her a squeeze I knew she wouldn't understand. It made her giggle.

"They really, really do," I said. "As long as you believe."

– Chuck Frederick, December 23, 2010

The author wishes to thank Konnie, Cindy, Paul, Siiri and everyone at *Lake Superior Magazine* for their belief in this project; Julie for her untiring support and her valuable input and feedback; and Claire, Charleigh and Reggie for their encouragement and bottomless well of love. The author also wishes to thank Marcia. Of course.

Photo Album

Alan at Troon Country Club in
Scottsdale, Arizona.

Shirley & Marcia at home.

Santa hangs out beside "Shirley's Tree".

WELCOME TO OUR HOLIDAY LIGHT FANTASY FEEL FREE TO WALK THROUGH THE DISPLAY ENJOY!

PLEASE WATCH YOUR STEP

A special shooting star honors young Ellie's bright life.

The firepit draws visitors (and even Marcia sometimes).

A swirl tree for Marcia's friend John Young and a nativity for all.

Shirley's in her red booties and
a peaceful, silent night.

*In the distance beyond the trees laps
the ever-present Lake Superior.*

Do you believe?

Another starry night with Marcia's Spirit in the Lights.